Sicily: The Trampled Paradise

Revisited

LEGAS

Sicilian Studies

Volume III

Series Editor: Gaetano Cipolla

Other volumes published in this series:

1. Giuseppe Quatriglio, *A Thousand Years in Sicily: from the Arabs to the Bourbons,* transl. by Justin Vitiello, 1992, 1997;
2. Henry Barbera, *Medieval Sicily: the First Absolute State,* 1994, 2000;
3. Connie Mandracchia DeCaro, *Sicily, the Trampled Paradise, Revisited,* 1998; 2008
4. Justin Vitiello, *Labyrinths and Volcanoes: Windings Through Sicily,* 1999;
5. Ben Morreale, *Sicily: The Hallowed Land*, 2000;
6. Joseph Privitera, *The Sicilians,* 2001;
7. Franco Nicastro and Romolo Menighetti, *History of Autonomous Sicily,* transl. by Gaetano Cipolla, 2002;
8. Maria Rosa Cutrufelli, *The Woman Outlaw,* transl. by Angela M. Jeannet, 2004;
9. Enzo Lauretta, *The Narrow Beach.* transl. by Giuliana Sanguinetti Katz and Anne Urbancic, 2004;
10. Venera Fazio and Delia De Santis, ed. *Sweet Lemons: Writings with a Sicilian Accent,* 2004;
11. *The Story of Sicily,* 2005. (Never printed)
12. Gaetano Cipolla, *Siciliana:Studies on the Sicilian Ethos*, 2005.
13. Paolo Fiorentino, *Sicily Through Symbolism and Myth,* 2006
14. Giacomo Pilati, *Sicilian Women,* 2008

CONNIE MANDRACCHIA DECARO

Sicily:
The Trampled Paradise

Revisited

Second Edition

LEGAS

Library of Congress Cataloging-in-Publication Data

De Caro, Connie Mandracchia, 1931 -
   Sicily the trampled paradise : revisited / Connie Mandracchia De Caro.
   p. c m. — (Sicilian Studies : v. 3)
   Includes bibliographical references and index.
   ISBN 1-881901-15-7
   1. Sicily (Italy) — History. 2. Mafia—Italy—Sicily—History. 3. Sicily (Italy)—Social conditions. I. Title. II. Seris.
   DG866.D39 1998
   945'.8—dc21
98-7778
                                                                        CIP

Printed and bound in Canada

Acknowledgments
   We are grateful to Rosanna Musotto Piazza for the use of her oil painting "San Mauro Castelverde" for the cover. From *Rosanna Musotto Piazza* (Milano: Giorgio Mondadori & Associati), 1989.
   (Rosanna Musotto Piazza, Via M.se di Villabianca, 4, 90143 Palermo)

For information and for orders, write to:
LEGAS

P.O. Box 149   3 Wood Aster Bay
Mineola, New York   Ottawa, Ontario
11501, USA   KIN 8T9 Canada
                          www.Legaspublishing.com

To my mother who inspired me

To Ari who listened

TABLE OF CONTENTS

PREFACE

An Appreciation

I gained much pleasure as well as useful information in reading Connie Mandracchia DeCaro's book on Sicily. For one thing, Sicily's history provides an excellent summary of what we know about the power struggles of Ancient times, and those between the Lords of the Middle Ages, and the royal houses of Europe thereafter, right up to the modern era, where royal ambition is replaced by the cynical calculations of realpolitik. However, seen from the vantage of the Sicilians, from their "trampled paradise," as DeCaro has aptly named it, Sicily's exploiters aren't memorable for their objectives, as they are in texts which explain the history of Europe in terms of alliances and battles, and the relative success or failure of dominant figures. Yes, we will learn of the strategic importance of Sicily in the larger context of Europe, of the tribute she had to pay, of the way absentee landlords neglected her natural resources or despoiled her of them, but the story DeCaro is most anxious to tell, as the last third of the book makes plain, is the story of the *Sicilian* people, whose land and labor was relentlessly appropriated by interests besides their own, a people who— though valiant in battle and heroic in resistance—were prevented in every conceivable way from having anything of their own to fight for. As the centuries go by and the regimes come and go and the abuses continue we begin to feel viscerally the depredations of prince and dictator and democracy alike, of their armies and their henchmen within Sicily, and we gain a new respect for the people who endured them.

Americans are accustomed to hearing about Sicily as the birthplace of the Mafia, and DeCaro has taken special pains to deal with history of this organization as well as to correct popular stereotypes that grossly misrepresent the actual "contribution" of Sicily to underworld activity in the United States. Avoiding both sensationalism and partisan defensiveness, she has presented as clear a picture as one is likely to find of the Mafia's rise, of its historical role in Sicilian society and of its embattled role in modern times.

Besides setting the record straight about the more visible but statistically insignificant criminal element in Sicily, DeCaro has presented a delightful portrait of the ordinary Sicilian citizen, showing how the bitter history of his island has left its mark on his character. Throughout, Decaro has scattered popular refrains in the Sicilian dialect, with adjacent English translations. Delightful to read for their wry insights, particularly in jabs at the people responsible for their condition, they also attest to a strain of fatalism which is equally a product of historical necessity.

The general reader will be entertained by this lively book; the reader of European history will be refreshed by the presentation of familiar history in an illuminating new context; the Italophile who wants to know more about his friends of Sicilian origin will be surprised at the scope of their history and curious about the way it has influenced strategies for living and traits of character; Italian Americans, and in particular Sicilian Americans will be delighted to have their story told by someone who fully appreciates its significance — who also happens to be a compassionate person and a graceful and insightful writer.

Jeff Putnam

Jeff Putnam is a novelist, screenwriter, biographer, translator and an opera singer specializing in the French and Italian repertory. He is author of the novels *Good Men, Bottoms Up, Sellout* and *By the Wayside* published as a tetralogy by Baskerville Publishers. He is presently working on a biography of Brazilian soprano Bidu Sayao, on a study of the life and art Amelita Galli-Curci and on a filmscript of his novel *Demigod*, to be screened as Devil's Advocate.

Introduction

As long as the civilized world centered around the Mediterranean Sea, Sicily remained the vital core of that civilized world. The island's strategic position in the Mediterranean, midway between the mainland of Italy, North Africa, and the eastern Mediterranean, determined the *leitmotifs* of its history. Its position encouraged settlement from all areas and its size allowed settlement from many invasions at once. Yet, Sicily was not large enough to present a serious threat to her conquering neighbors from Africa, the East, and Europe. This island, 25,000 sq. km., less than 1/3 the size of Ireland and 1/4 the size of Cuba, was too small to defend itself against attack by the myriads that landed on its shores through the centuries. In fact, having had very few peaceful periods of self-government in its long history, Sicily was denied fulfillment of the political, economic, and social potential that results from the harmonic crescendo of a united people working in concert.

On the contrary, with foreign dominations, the island became a battlefield for foreign armies. Wealth and resources were appropriated, the land and people were exploited, and nothing was returned to the land or its people, therefore imposing grave harm to both. Destined to be a territory of innumerable invasions, Sicily was denied the shaping of its own history and was instead subjected to the history of its invaders.

The flood of migrations and invasions in the course of its ancient, medieval, and modern history was relentless, yet the consequences have remained inadequately recognized and comprehended. The first settlers to arrive were anonymous prehistoric people; then came the Sicans, Sicels, Phoenicians, Elymi, Greeks, Romans, Vandals, Byzantines, Arabs, Normans, Swabians, French, Spaniards, and Austrians. The majority of these remained and contributed in different ways to a continuous biological and cultural fusion which, through the centuries, resulted in an extraordinary blend of people with no group identifiably dominant over the other. Tragically, through centuries of domination, a dangerous fragmentation occurred within this society which was so deprived of liberty and patriotic ideals that any attempt at national identity and unity was doomed. A dangerous polarization resulted. Most harmful of all was the negative social ambience which the Sicilians had little hand in shaping. Only their tenacious resiliency and resourcefulness have enabled them to survive the ages of turmoil.

For much of its history the island was a region of extraordinary fertility where grain, olive trees, grapevines, fruit trees, and beauty of landscape abounded. There was an abundance of forests rich with oak, chestnut, pine, and fir trees. After centuries of foreign wars on Sicilian soil, exploitation and neglect, very little of the land remained woodland. Fundamental damage done resulted in drastic deforestation which changed not only the island's appearance, but, even worse, its ecological balance. Many of the island's streams dried and none of its rivers was navigable any longer. By the end of the last century, after countless heroic attempts at independence, disillusionment with Italian unification and subsequent severe economic crises, this region, that had for so many centuries attracted mass migrations and invasions, became associated with mass emigration as a great numbers of its people began to pull away in search of a future.

Only today does one begin to see a return to the beauty of the distant past as Sicily, now an autonomous region, nurtures its citizens proudly, through self-determination, towards the attainment of its ancestral dream of independence, honor, fruitful labor, love of family and love of "patria".

Prehistory

Although Sicily was inhabited from remote prehistoric times, the earliest origin of its people is tenuously traced. It is believed that the first inhabitants arrived by sea about 20,000 years B.C., during the Upper Paleolithic period. This migration of Cro-Magnons brought stone tools and utensils and left artistic incisions for posterity in the Addaura caves of Monte Pellegrino and the island of Levanzo, near Trapani. Interest in Sicilian Paleolithic art erupted after important archeological excavations in the 1950s unearthed exciting works, considered to be among the finest examples of the period. Wall decorations discovered in Levanzo consist of incised and painted scenes of animals and anthropomorphic figures. The incised figures, in excellent perspective, are lively and naturalistic. A particularly appealing engraving, the figure of a young doe turning its head, is considered by Prof. Bernabò Brea,[1] one of Europe's most distinguished archeologists, to be among the most beautiful expressions of Quaternary art in Sicily. In Monte Pellegrino the groupings are unusual and complex and consist of numerous human figures, some revealing movements of subtle eroticism.

Of particular interest is the discovery of a series of incised drawings in the Addaura caves on the northern side of Monte Pellegrino (Palermo) where human figures were depicted as well as those of animals, as in Quatenary art. One incised group forms a complex scene of 10 male figures, some of whom seem to be dancing in a ring around two reclining figures, as another is moving towards them carrying a long spear. Some of the dancers have arms raised in dance-like gestures.[2] According to Prof. Brea, the discovery of the engravings at Levanzo and Addaura raised Sicily to a position of the first magnitude in the study of Paleolithic culture in Europe.

During the Upper Paleolithic period, the inhabitants of Sicily were producing large numbers of microlithic implements, geometric in shape, which were discovered in archeologic sites near Messina. Geometric microliths and microblades (small flints) were inserted on arrows, spears, and sickles as well as in other bone or wooden implements and used for hunting and procuring other food.

The Paleolithic period, the earliest and longest stage of human cultural development, which spanned about two and a half million years, came to an end circa 8,500 B.C. Global warming, circa 10,000 B.C., resulted in the retreat of glaciers to the highest mountains and a rising of sea level. Lakes and rivers replaced the glaciers, and forests replaced the steppes of southeast Europe and Asia and the tundras of the Arctic region.

During the Mesolithic period, in a now warm climate, people fished with nets and hooks, caught birds, and gathered cereals. A great change in natural surroundings occurred in a few millenia which led to a cultural revolution. Cultivation of wheat and barley and the domestication of food animals such as sheep, goats, pigs, and cattle occurred between 9,000 and 5,000 B.C. The earliest evidence has been found, thus far, in the Fertile Crescent in the Near East and in southern Anatolia. As climatic changes occurred, periods of enormous migrations throughout the Mediterranean shores also emerged.

By 5,000 B.C. the first peasant communities were established. The change from a hunting-and-gathering economy to one based on food production ushered in the Neolithic period and sedentism (early settled life in stable communities).

By 5,000 B.C. a general transformation of the central Mediterranean region resulted in the appearance of more evolved communities where the use of stone tools continued, but with the addition of farming, cattle raising, and ceramic arts. It is believed that this migration spread along the Mediterranean from the coastal regions of northern Syria and southern Anatolia, across the Balkan Peninsula to France, and Spain, and south along the Italian peninsula, across the strait of Messina to Sicily, and on to North Africa. The inhabitants of the island navigated along the coast in small vessels, sailing far enough to trade their products. They lived in huts fortified by surrounding ditches cut in soft limestone backed by dirt ramparts. The huts were grouped together in villages. Their stone tools of basalt and obsidian were now polished, and their ceramic utensils were decorated with engravings before firing. Lances used for hunting had propellants which extended their range farther than that of the human arm. Slings were used to facilitate hunting. The dead were buried in rock within caves.

Traces of this more advanced civilization have been found in Stentinello, near Syracuse, and in Serraferlicchio, near Agrigento. According to Prof. Brea, "the Stentinello pottery fits perfectly, both technically and stylistically, into this wider complex of impressed pottery, and it is perhaps one of its most artistically advanced developments."[3] (See p. 127, illustrations) Artifacts found in Stentinello include many shards of three-color ware decorated with bordered red stripes and complicated scroll handles which are considered artistically advanced. Interestingly, Sicily's Neolithic ceramics industry underwent a parabolic evolution. The earliest products were mono-chromatic, followed by more decorative two colors. Then a degree of so-phistication was achieved as three colors and decorative meanders and spi-rals were used, which became richer and heavier, and handles became larger and more complicated.(See illustration on p.131) Finally, colors were re-placed by monochrome glossy-red, and handles became schematic. A de-cline in technique and artistic quality became evident in the late Neolithic Diana Culture unearthed near Adrano (Mineo), in the southeast part of the island. Ceramic art of the glossy-red Diana style and the two- and three-color finer pottery of the previous Stentinello culture were found as far north as Umbria, Marche and Tuscany, leading Professor Brea to conclude that commercial exchanges were already active through southern Italy and Sic-ily as early as the late Neolithic period.[4]

Metallurgy was practiced in eastern Anatolia more than 10,000 years ago, but, initially, metals such as copper were treated like stone and beaten into shape with stones. The earliest known artifacts made by the smelting of copper date from about 3,500 B.C. in Iran.By 3,000 B.C. bronze implements were in common use in the Near East. During this era, large groups of IndoEuropean speaking people began to appear along the shores of the Mediterranean basin spurred on by a search for minerals. Travel to distant lands had become reality with the development of new vessels that could face the open sea beyond Italy and Sicily to Sardinia, France, and Spain. An enormous social and ethnical revolution occurred. A rapid mixing of groups occurred as male travelers took indigenous females as mates.

During the late Neolithic period, *circa* 4,000 B.C., large migrations occurred across the eastern Balkans onto the mainland of Italy; among these, it seems, were the Sicels followed by the Sicans. Sicans and Sicels were probably similar peoples, both speaking an IndoEuropean language.[5] They settled in an area later known as southern Etruria, Lazio, and Campania. Some archeologists have traced the Sicel migration back to the Cyclades (Naxos) and Athens. Yet similarities have been found to Italic and Latin populations, including many common elements of language. The Sicans preceded the Sicels in their journey to Sicily. Archeologists have traced their steps south as they were shouldered out by the Sicels, who in turn left their "footprints" on their journey to Sicily (Late Bronze, Early Iron Age).

From the necropoli of antiquity, archeologists are able to formulate a reality which otherwise would remain forever lost to us. As cultures are unearthed and understood, they are attributed to the different peoples populating the areas under scrutiny. As cremation (incineration) cultures practiced in southern Italy and Sicily are traced to Eastern cultures, the *Fossakulture,* burial in underground tombs, is attributed to Sicel culture. The most conspicuous traces of this culture are found in the territory we know to have been inhabited by Sicels before they were forced to search for a new habitat in the South. Besides Populonia, Vetulonia, Tarquinia, Falerii and Terni in the Etruscan area and in Umbria, underground tombs were found in Rome and preHellenic Ischia, Nola, Nocera, preHellenic Locri and eastern Sicily. [6] From these underground tombs, where the dead were buried in supine position and no longer in fetal position of earlier times, burial dowries were unearthed that were more valuable than the poor dowries found in cremation tombs.[7] In later millennia, in underground tombs of the Villanova civilization of central Italy, richer dowries were found. Then centuries later, in Etruscan necropoli, a wealth of luxurious gifts was unearthed.

By 3,000 B.C., after a long migration, the Sicans arrived on the island from the mainland and settled in eastern Sicily. Later they moved to the central and southwestern part of the island. Recent excavations in Camico, in the province of Agrigento, where it is thought that they lived, reveal urban centers placed strategically on hills, and large tombs containing an abundance of ceramics, such as engraved vases, some painted in red, with geometric motifs. Gold objects and rings with bezels engraved with figures of animals, such as the wolf or the cow milking its calf, were also found. (The legend of Icarus and Daedalus is firmly rooted in Camico, the legendary town built by and lived in by Daedalus.[8]) Much later, with the arrival of the Phoenicians and the Greeks, the Sicans came under their influence, yet they are mentioned as a distinct people as late as the 4th century B.C.

During the late Copper, early Bronze Ages (c.2nd millenium) the Castelluccio culture flourishing in southeastern (Syracuse, Ragusa, Gela) to midsouthern (Agrigento) Sicily revealed hundreds of oven-shaped rock tombs, some with doors, some with entry vestibules with four pillars, and some containing grave goods. This culture was characterized by a variety of graceful ceramic utensils with painted brown or black lines on light yellow or reddish background, sometimes enhanced with white strokes. Decorative motifs were frequently repeated. The bronze industry included blades of extraordinary length and perfection. Numerous ornamental beads and pendants and extremely fine quality schematized idols have been found which according to Mr. Brea "show skilled craftmanship and are considered the most perfect creations of Sicilian prehistory."[9] (See pp. 128-30, illustrations) The Castelluccio culture seems not to have had any affinity with that of the Italian peninsula. According to Prof. Brea it had Aegeo-Anatolian characteristics and was flourishing on the island long before the Sicels crossed over into Sicily.

By 1300 B.C., many of the Sican towns had moved further uphill on more defendable locations as protection against a threatening migration arriving from the mainland. Peaceful and commercial exchanges among the various Mediterranean peoples were greatly curtailed and the prosperous civilization that Sicily and the Aeolian Islands enjoyed during the Early and Middle Bronze Age ended. A time of war and fear began, an army was raised to resist the attack of the Sicels arriving from the Italian peninsula. The Sicels, also IndoEuropean speaking, defeated the Sicans and settled in the eastern part of the island as the Sicans retreated to more remote areas of the island.

The Sicilian Bronze and Early Iron Age has been closely identified with the Sicels. Recent thrilling and enlightening excavations have unearthed a wealth of artifacts known as the Pantalica culture which spanned 1250 B.C. to the end of the 8th century B.C.[10] Since Pantalica is the largest excavated habitation site of this period, its name has been given to this East Sicilian civilization. The Pantalica plateau towers above the surrounding valleys making it a natural fortress. Very little is yet known of habitations except for the prince's palace, built of large polygonal blocks in megalithic construction. In various excavations in the area of Pantalica, bronze tools of remarkable accuracy, flame- shaped blades, razors, mirrors, and elegant fibulae used to fasten cloaks have been unearthed. Graceful, socketed axes, spear fragments, and ingots of bronze have also been found. Sicel ceramics of this period were elegant, colorful, and shaped on the wheel. Chamber type tombs of small oven-shaped rooms cut into rock continued. The architecture of the tombs and the prestigious funerary gifts (such as gold rings) support the hypothesis of politically prominent groups in proto-urban settlements involved in the commerce of metals, utilizing workshops which specialized in the production of bronze objects and ceramics shaped on the wheel.[11] (See illustrations on pp. 131-4).

An archeological site near Adrano on the lower slopes of Mt. Etna, at present almost unexplored, has yielded the most important inscriptions in the Sicel language thus far, along with the biggest hoard of bronzes yet found in Sicily, dating back to circa 850-730 B.C. A good many words of the Sicel language are already known and nearly all of them are considered closely related to Latin. *Fibulae* and other bronzes from this area near Adrano show that this site was already in existence at least at the time of Pantalica South (850-730 B.C.).[12]

Little has been determined of the provenance of the enigmatic settlers of Erice and Segesta in western Sicily, but several theories are available. According to Thucydides, the Elymi had escaped from Troy during the Trojan War in the 12th century B.C. Another Greek historian, Hellanicus, of the 6th century B.C. tells us that the Elymi descended from Liguria on the mainland shortly before the arrival of the Sicels. In very recent years, excavations around old Segesta have unearthed thousands of minute ceramic fragments dating from the 8th century, B.C. Varnished ceramic shards marked with graffiti consisting of letters, fragments of words, or a word or two were found. According to glottologists, these words were written in Greek letters, but they belonged to a non-Greek language. According to some, the language is Anatolic of Hittite origin. Others are convinced that two invasions occurred in western Sicily between the end of the second millennium and the start of the first, one from the Aegean and the other from Lucania and Bruzio (Abbruzzi province) in the mainland of Italy. Although the Elymi were culturally close to the Greeks, they were politically allied to the Carthaginians who were enemies of the Greeks.

An Island of Promise for the Greeks

In 735 B.C. Greek embarkations sailed into a harbor on the east coast of Sicily and established a town which they named Naxos. The wealth and beauty of the island must have attracted them in their search for a new home-land. It was such a paradise of forests, grain, and fruit orchards that it later came to be called "the land of Demeter". Commercial exchanges had been occurring for centuries between the islanders and the Hellenic neighbor to the East. The explorers found an island where vast areas of woods had al-ready been cleared and planted. They eventually introduced the cultivation of the olive tree and perhaps of vineyards, too. They improved cultivation of pre-existing almond and other fruit trees. They found existing communi-ties and, among the inhabitants, women who helped them to create new lives on the land.

In fact, four ethnic groups shared the island. Phoenicians, newly ar-rived from the city of Tyre (Middle East, perhaps Lebanon) had settled a colony in North Africa which they named Carthage (present Tunisia). They spread their influence establishing ports of call on northwestern beaches of Sicily in the 9th century B.C. Sicans had arrived in the 3rd millennium B.C. from the peninsula of Italy, settling in the East. They later occupied an area, Camico, adjacent to Selinunte and Agrigento, in southwest Sicily. Sicels, too, had settled in Sicily by the end of the 2nd millennium B.C. and settled along the eastern and south-eastern coast. The Elymi (provenance question-able, possibly the mainland or Troy) were settled in Segesta and Erice.[13]

Greek expansion resulted in vast migrations of Ionic[15] and then Doric[16] populations to Sicily. Theirs became a race to conquer the island. Naxos was founded in 735 B.C. by the Chalcidonians.[17] The Corinthians,[18] and Megarians[19] settled Syracuse and Megara Iblea. In subsequent years, colo-nists from Crete and Rhodes founded Gela. Colonization spread: Naxos founded Catania and Messina and then Imera; Gela established Agrigento; and Megara Iblea founded Seli-nunte, both in Carthaginian and Sican terri-tory, around 628 B.C., to serve as a bulwark of Hellenism.

Despite its Greekness, Selinunte maintained its relations with its Carthaginian and Sican neighbors for almost two hundred years, until the defeat of the Carthaginians at the battle of Imera in 480 B.C. by Gelone,[20] the tyrant of Syracuse, who ruled the strongest Greek-Sicilian city in Sicily. By the middle of the 5th century, B.C., the Hellenization of the island was almost complete. Of the native Sicels, many had mingled with colonists creating Greek-Sicilian(Siceliot) centers and others gradually settled in more remote areas of the island. The degree of interchange among settlers and Sicels is evidenced by the intelligence and ease with which Greek (silver drachma) and Sicel (bronze litra) monetary systems were combined. A ratio was created to allow the two currencies to circulate simply.

Greek settlements, which had first been oligarchies of vast landowners, later alternated between democratic and monarchic regimes. Monarchies were led by the so-called "tyrants." Popular uprisings occurred but attempts to expel the "tyrants" failed. Territorial conflicts among Greek colonies and their Carthaginian and Sicel neighbors were frequent. The irredentist movement among Sicels, which had found its spokesman in their leader, Ducetius, also failed after his defeat and death in 444 B.C.

Many Sicels on the coast mingled with Greeks, but in inland towns they worked at retaining their independence. By optimizing the ethnic and religious bond which united the Sicels, Ducetius, a leader, attempted to create the independent Sicel state of Menainon (present-day Mineo) by uniting most of the Sicel towns under his leadership. The old sanctuary at the Lake of the Palici became the rallying ground for his troops. Ducetius led his army into battle against the Greeks in Syracuse, successfully capturing several towns along the way. After a decade of victories, his fortune changed and he and his army were defeated. He offered his life in exchange for leniency towards his men whom he wished to save from torture or death. His life was spared and he was sent into exile to Corinth instead. He did return to Sicily and succeeded in establishing a colony at Calatte (present-day Caronia), but he died soon after, and opportunity for freedom ended rapidly. Eventually Sicel opposition came to an end. They gradually came under Greek influence, adopted Greek ways and spoke Greek until the arrival of the Romans, who considered them Greeks too.

Sicel religious tradition made its way into Greek mythology. Theirs was the worship of the powers of nature and, above all worship of the gods of the underworld, the Palici, whom the Sicels felt were awe-inspiring but kindly. The Greeks did not alter this myth, except to invent parents for these Sicel gods, making them children of Zeus and the nymph, Thaleia. The Sicels believed that worshippers of Hybla were especially trained to interpret dreams. In the temple of Hadranus near Etna (and near present-day Mineo) the Sicels kept an eternal flame which, as legend has it, was guarded by 1000 dogs who welcomed the worthy and drove away the evil-doers, according to their sins. An oath taken there was the most binding of all oaths, and it was believed that a breach of that vow resulted in the sinner being torn to pieces by the dogs. To the present day, "chi ti manciassiru li cani!" ("the dogs should eat you!") is the malediction reserved for evildoers. The Sicel goddesses of the Earth who sent up fruitful corn lost their identity as they became absorbed into the Greek legend of Demeter and Persephone. Kalimathos, the Greek poet, and the Romans Cicero and Livy wrote of Enna, Sicily, as the home of Demeter and Persephone.[21]

As Hellenization on the island was taking place in Sicily, Athens was desperately defending its territory in destructive battles against the invading Persian army, under the command of General Xerxes. With the Persian army's defeat in 479 B.C., Athens eventually became embroiled in what is known as the Peloponnesian War, a war between Athenian and Spartan coalitions. Endless battles followed and cities were destroyed. By 417 B.C., the pro-Athenian democratic faction had regained control in Argos providing Athens with a much needed strong ally, while Sparta's leadership of the Peloponnese had been restored. Unwisely, in the Spring of 414 B.C. Athens launched an expedition to Sicily. Athenians had sent small fleets to Sicily earlier in the war to protect their allies there and expand their influence. The aim this time was the conquest of the entire island. Athenian conviction was that once powerful Syracuse was seized, the entire island would quickly fall, and thus they would expand their Empire. The siege of Syracuse started promisingly enough but conquest did not follow as expected. The recall of Arcibiades, the first ship's general, to face trial for treason in Athens, the death of Lamachus, the second ship's general while in battle with the Syracuse, and the arrival of the Spartan general, Gylippus, in Sicily to aid the city, turned the tide of battle against the Athenian invaders. Despite the arrival from Athens of a second fleet commanded by Demosthenes to aid General Nicia and his men, restoring Athenian spirits for a time, the commanders realized that the Athenian position had become untenable. The Athenian fleet was made ready to sail for home only to be defeated in Syracuse's Great Harbor. The invasion ended in defeat in 413 B.C. with 7,000 Athenian prisoners left to die of deprivation and starvation in the rock caves of Syracuse.

With Hellenic Sicily weakened in a war to retain its independence from Greece, the Carthaginian army took advantage of the favorable moment, came out of the northwest, and attacked and defeated Himera (Termini Imerese) in 409 B.C. Siceliot cities favored their city of origin and often reverted back to their provenance for assistance. Doric Selinunte, in her search for an ally, turned towards Doric Syracuse for help. Segesta, alarmed by the new alliance between Syracuse and Doric Selinunte turned for assistance to Ionic Athens already at war with Doric Sparta. Athens agreed to defend Segesta against their common enemy, the Dorians and for more than a century fierce battles raged between the two nations.

Agathocles was born, during this turbulent century, in 361 B.C. in Himera. He moved to Syracuse around 343 B.C. and served in the army. Later, he married a wealthy widow. He revealed his ambitions early and he was twice banished by Syracusans for attempting to overthrow their oligarchy. He returned with an army of mercenaries in 317 B.C., ostensibly to restore democracy to the city, but, in fact, his army massacred thousands of people and banished thousands. As "tyrant" of Syracuse, he was absolute ruler. ("Tyrant" did not then carry the negative implication it does today though it did imply absolute rule by a single individual.) Sicily's Siceliot cities and the Carthaginians frequently continued their war. Agathocles was defeated in 311 B.C. at the battle of Himera by the Carthaginians. Unwilling to accept defeat, he invaded northern Africa in 310 B.C. and a truce was signed four years later. In his final years, he restored democracy to Syracuse and did achieve some popularity. Agathocles died in 289 B.C. His successor was challenged with internal strife involving the Carthaginians again and later by mercenaries known as Mammertines.

After a century of war against the Carthaginians, Syracuse, in 298 B.C. summoned Pyrrhus, the King of Hellenistic Epirius, whom they knew to be fighting the Romans in Taranto for help against their enemy. Roman legions had been battling in Taranto, in the boot of Italy, against Pyrrhus, there to defend the city. Pyrrhus had arrived on the southern shore of Taranto in 281 B.C. with 20 elephants, 25,000 to 30,000 men to defend his fellow-Greek speaking Italiots in Magna Graecia. After much bloodshed between the two warring armies, an agreement was reached concerning exchange of prisoners of war and a period of armistice was begun. (Since 508 B.C. when the new Roman Republic had agreed on a treaty with Carthage, relations had become tolerable between the two states. In 306 B.C. they had further strengthened their relations with reciprocal recognition of a Roman sphere of influence in Italy and a Carthaginian influence in Sicily, Sardinia, and Corsica. But the expanding Roman Empire would not remain for long without Sicily in its conquest of all Magna Graecia.)

Replying to Syracuse's appeal, Pyrrhus placed a garrison in Taranto and left for Sicily, angering the inhabitants of Taranto who demanded that he complete what they had paid him to do. Once in Sicily, Pyrrhus, whose memoirs on the art of war were later quoted by many ancient authors, including Cicero, recruited and trained an army from Syracuse of about 45,000 men. He advanced to Mt. Erice in northwest Sicily and routed the Carthaginians who were then forced to negotiate. While negotiating, Pyrrhus dealt with another enemy, the Mammertimes, former mercenaries who, earlier, had been in the pay of Agathocles of Syracuse supporting him until his death, and, then, they, themselves, had occupied Messina. He attacked Messina and to some degree defeated the Mammertines. Pyrrhus succeeded in occupying most of the island but was unable to rout the Carthaginians from Lilibeo (Marsala) and finally returned to Greece. The carnage resulting from these battles gave rise to the ironic "Pyrrhic victory".

Syracuse attacked Messina to reclaim it and the Mammertines turned for help to their Roman neighbors garrisoned in Reggio. Syracuse, soon aware of imminent destruction by Roman forces arriving on Sicilian soil, ironically turned to its age-old enemy, the Carthaginians, for help against a common enemy! Soon all that had been Sicel, Greek, Elymi, Carthaginian, that is, Sicilian by way of assimilation, disappeared in the face of the bloody conflict fought on the island by its inhabitants and the invading Romans. Finally, in 277 B.C. Rome took control. Sicily lost its independence and became a Roman province.

A high level of civilization was attained in Sicily during the five centuries of Greek-Sicilian (Siceliot) co-existence. Magna Grecia (Great Greece)was in its fullest cultural, economic and political flowering during the 6th century B.C. Dr. Claudio De Palma, professor of Etruscan archeology at the University of Florence, disagrees with the concept that the development of Italiot and Siceliot colonies remained culturally dependent on the mother-cities in Greece. He states that traditions and advanced culture were brought by the Greeks to their new land but these were quickly absorbed in the rapid autonomous development of the new communities.[24] Settlers began to build settlements with a planned, functional perspective. In Greece, towns continued to evolve helter-skelter. In Sicily a completely different type of city emerged. Dr. Malcolm Bell, professor of archaeology at the American Academy in Rome, says "Until the early 1970s we were taught that urban planning was invented at the city of Piraeus in mainland Greece in 430 B.C.; Megara Hyblaea shows us it happened in Sicily about three centuries earlier." In the 8th century B.C., the settlers of Megara Hyblaea, who were among the first to arrive, built their houses clearly laid out on a grid of streets. Different sectors of the city served different functions.

A rapid economic, cultural, and exceptional artistic flowering occurred within the first decades of the Greek migration which exhibited many original and independent characteristics if compared to parallel developments in

Greece. Dr. Di Palma stresses the fact that in the 7th and 6th centuries B.C., the periods that in art history are called *eastern* and *archaic*, Athens was not yet the model of civilization for the Greek world and its satellites that it became in the 5th century B.C. The two poles around which intellectual, artistic, and commercial exchanges among Greeks or Greek speaking people gravitated were Anatolia and Magna Graecia together with eastern and southern Sicily.[25] Sir Moses I. Finley, the historian and author of *A History of Sicily*, states that a flow of traffic continued between the Greek world and Sicily. Once established in their new land, patrons invited poets, architects, and philosophers to the island, and their Siceliot counterparts visited Greece. Siceliots consulted the Oracle at Delphi and participated in the Olympic games.

The brilliant flowering of commerce, art, law, literature, building arts, and ornamental arts in Sicily reached its apex during the 5th century B.C. The awe-inspiring archeological remains scattered everywhere around the island, at Syracuse, Gela, Agrigento, Selinunte, Imera, and Segesta attest to the greatness of the era. An independent spirit appeared in the spectacular temples of Sicily and Magna Graecia. Western temple builders experimented freely with design, becoming architectural leaders. The Temple of Athena in Poseidonia, south of Naples, combined simple Doric with the more elaborate Ionic style. Architects in Greece would not blend those two rigidly observed styles for 50 years.

According to Sir Moses I. Finley, since Sicily lacked metals, the colonization of the island was otherwise motivated by a desire to make a new life on the land. This westward movement from Greece was organized by various cities to encourage and sometimes compel men to move out permanently to new and independent communities of their own. Details are lacking, he continues, because although Greeks had become literate by this time, having borrowed and improved the Phoenician alphabet, they did not keep historical records. Consequently, their own traditions about the opening up of Sicily and the West, preserved in Greek writings of later centuries, are not satisfactory since they are a combination of mythology and heroic legend rather than history.[26]

Among the most illustrious names of the Siceliot period were: Epicarmus of Syracuse (528-431 B.C.), who gave artistic unity to comedy; Empedocles of Agrigento (490-430 B.C.), physician and philosopher; Timeo of Taormina (350-280 B.C.), historian; Teocritus of Syracuse (315-240 B.C.), poet of the pastoral life. The dominant name is Archimedes of Syracuse (287-212 B.C.), physics and mathematics genius, and builder of machines and military equipment.

Prof. Santo Correnti cites the historian, Biagio Pace, of the University of Rome, who stressed in *Arte e Civiltà della Sicilia Antica,* 1938, the originality of Siceliot plastic art when compared to models of Hellenic art, and the philologist, Quintino Catandella, of the University of Genova, in his *History of Greek Literature,* 1953, who demonstrated the originality of Siceliot poets like Stesicoro in their philosophical interpretations of the Greek myths when compared to Greek models. In 1952, the French author, Roger Peyrefitte, affirmed that Greek-Sicily was the most dazzling center of civilization in the Mediterranean world, and the Sicilian poet, the 1959 Nobel Prize recipient, Salvatore Quasimodo, wrote that "the best Sicilian blood nourished the civilization of Pericles's Age."[27] The customary method of referring to the island's exceptional patrimony bears the stigma of a domination never fully identified with the dominated area. That explains why, even today, one speaks of Greek monuments in Sicily, traces of Arab architecture in Sicily, Norman castles in Sicily, and so on, forgetting that these are, by full right, manifestations of Sicilian culture.

Since so much of the glory of the past has been usurped by historians on the side of the conquerors, it seems to this writer that to usurp on the side of the vanquished is also presumptuous, but a fusion of past glories is long overdue and more than just; therefore the words, *Italiot* and *Siceliot* for Greek Italian and Greek Sicilian seem most appropriate and distinctive.

The Breadbasket of Rome / Christianity

The battle to conquer Sicily resulted in carnage and destruction. In fact, Sicily became the battlefield for the bloody conflict between two giants, Rome and Carthage. With Roman troops within throwing distance on the southern tip of Italy and the Sicilian city of Messina revolting against the Carthaginians, Rome realized its opportune moment to intervene by defending the Sicilian city against its attackers, and the first Punic War erupted in 264 B.C. ('Peoni' is Latin for Phoenician.) It was fought entirely on Sicilian soil. Battles raged and cities were destroyed. Romans besieged cities under Carthaginian control. Carthage attempted to strike back with its naval might only to be defeated. At last, Carthage surrendered Sicily and paid an indemnity to Rome to cover war expenses. Following its defeat in the first Punic War, Carthage turned to rebuilding its strength by expanding its empire in Spain. Rome would again, in 218 B.C. face its Carthaginian enemy, who had become, by then, a far more formidable power on its own homeland.

Under Roman rule, the island was subjected to systematic exploitation as booty of war. Battles raged and cities were destroyed by the Romans who sold the inhabitants of these cities into slavery: 25,000 inhabitants from Akragas (Agrigento), 13,000 from Palermo, and thousands from other cities. To save themselves from slavery many thousands of citizens were forced to pay ransom to thei conquorers. At the end of the 3rd century B.C., with the bloodshed of battle over and Rome the victor, the last traces of independence in Sicily were destroyed, and its economic connections with the outside world became Roman as the island became an appendage of Rome.

As a province of Rome, payment of tributes which were shipped to Rome, one-tenth of wheat and barley crops, was imposed upon the islanders. Others taxes were levied on wine, olives, fruit and vegetables.

His, however, was not the end of taxes. In addition to those paid directly to Rome, Sicilians paid their own local taxes, the cost of their water supply, festivals, maintenance of public buildings, yet they had no right to conduct foreign affairs, and were denied their own militia. Boding ill above all else was the economic inequality resulting from the creation of vast estates given by Roman decree to a privileged few from the mainland. Large, landless, and unemployed classes emerged, whose condition was worsened by vast numbers of newly imported slaves from the East. Sicily was on its way to becoming a land of large estates known as latifondi. The island, rich in wooded areas, was otherwise completely cultivated and orchards, gardens filled the spaces between latifondi and pastures. Whatever influence Rome had on Sicily, it must be remembered that in many ways the peninsula remained a foreign country. All Sicilians spoke Greek as their mother tongue while Latin was considered a foreign language, at least until the end of the first century B.C.

A period of struggle for control of the island followed the assassination of Julius Caesar in 44 B.C. as Sextus, the son of Pompey, placed on the proscription list by the Triumvirs, Anthony Octavian and Lepidus, selected Sicily as his escape route. He captured Messina and Syracuse and other cities surrendered without a struggle. Within a short period, Sextus had become a major force in the civil war between Brutus and Cassius and the Triumvirs. It was strengthened by a group of his father's followers who hoped he would lead them in saving the Republic.

To aid Sextus in his cause was the great influx of slaves who manned the ships which gave Sextus control of the seas. He forced a blockade on Rome and the rest of the peninsula denying supplies from Sicily and other areas as well. In 39 B.C. the Triumvirs agreed to grant Sextus authority in Sicily, Corsica, and Sardinia, and granted freedom to slaves in his service. Sextus agreed to lift the blockade, resume shipment of tithes and deny fugitive slaves entry onto the island. Peace was temporary and disputes quickly arose which led to further war. Damage was extensive, hundreds of warships were destroyed. Cities agreeing to surrender were granted pardon and others were sacked. Octavian had control of the Empire by 31 B.C.

It was during the reign of Emperor Octavian, 27 B.C. – 14B.C. that a period of peace began and Sicily became the breadbasket of the Empire. Agricultural production was varied and intensified and commerce was extended. The island remained ecologically sound, its fertile fields plentifully cultivated, and communication with the inland improved as better roads were built. However, the island's well-being remained an unknown. Land and wealth were in the hands of very few landholders, many of whom had come from Rome or southern Italy to occupy the fertile plains given to them. Since the Romans taxed excessively and took the island's wealth back with them to Rome very little remained for the island.

Sicily had become an appendage of Rome, and Sicels, Carthaginians, Elymi, and Greeks (Siceliots) became subjects of Roman conquest and Roman rule. Until the end of the 1st century B.C., Greek remained the mother tongue as the culture of the island remained prevalently Greek, while Latin was considered a foreign language. Latinization and the spread of Christianity, including the establishment of the first Christian church in the West, became the two dominant forces during this period. Eventually, Latin became the literary language in all of Sicily and came to be used for official writings. But the Greek language was tenacious. Not even in the western and northwestern sections of the island, which had not had a long Greek history, was the populace completely Latinized. The dividing line between these two languages seems to have been social. The majority of the population remained Greek- speaking, while the administrative and cultured minority spoke Latin or were bilingual.[28]

Judaism was diffused in Sicily by the 1st century B.C. Christian doctrine was introduced and spread rapidly from the 2nd to the 4th centuries, initially on the east coast (Catania and Syracuse), where St. Paul visited. The Christian catacombs in Syracuse, Agrigento, Noto, Marsala, Palermo, and Catania predate 200 A.D. by just a few years and attest to the spread of the new faith. The first Christian church of Europe was founded in Syracuse in the Doric Temple of Athena, which today is the cathedral of the city. Initially the spread of Christianity was almost overlooked and not considered a threat to pagan Rome. It soon became apparent that it could not be stopped, nor ignored, by the Empire. It was becoming a powerful entity to be reckoned with if the Empire's unity was to continue.

Rapidly spreading in its sphere of influence among its pagan population, Christianity had created a backlash of danger for followers of the new faith. In the year 284 A.D. Emperor Diocletian rose to power and issued severe edicts and punishments against Christians. As numbers increased, countless Sicilian Christians were made martyrs to their religion. In the 3rd century A.D. Sts. Agata and Lucy chose martyrdom rather than renunciation of their faith. St. Agata was born in Catania and martyred in circa 250 A.D. According to legend, she rejected the advances of a Roman prefect, and as a result was persecuted by him for her devotion to Christianity. Refusing renunciation, she was tortured and finally put to death. She became the patron saint of Catania. Thirty years later, in Syracuse, Lucy was born into a wealthy family. Legend relates that when Lucy came to the notice of watchful spies and was reported to authorities she, too, refused to renounce her faith. She plucked out her own eyes before she was put to death.

Nevertheless, the spread of Christianity could not be stopped and could no longer be ignored by the Empire. In May, 304 A.D. Emperor Diocletian abdicated and persecutions diminished. In 313 A.D., in Milano, Emperor Constantine's Edict of Milan granted tolerance towards Christianity. At last new avenues were opened to Christians for greater acceptance in society. It is thought that Constantine, too, converted to Christianity and became a great patron of the Church. Pagan temples were converted into churches and the Papacy acquired land. It was after the Edict of Milan that a rapid spread of the religion was seen in Sicily.

By the 7th century, four Sicilians had been popes, St. Agatone (678-81), St. Leone II (681-83), Conone (686-87), and St. Sergio I (687-701), whose verbal confrontations with the Byzantine emperor, Justinian II, brought him renown. Another Sicilian pope, St. Stefano IV (816-17), followed Pope Leo III who crowned Charlemagne, in 800 A.D.; St. Stefano IV had an important role in the confrontation between Charlemagne and the Longobards.[29]

The Barbarians / The Byzantines

The dismemberment of the Roman Empire was completed over a period of two hundred years. The political division was accomplished under Diocletian, Roman Emperor from 284-305 A.D. By establishing an autocratic government he laid the groundwork to allow the Empire to continue to control half the known world for almost two centuries. By modifying the structure of imperial government, he helped stabilize the Empire economically and militarily. After several years of rule, he had concluded that the Empire was too vast for a single emperor to control. One ruler alone could not address barbarian invasions on the Rhine and Egyptian disputes in the South simultaneously. He decided to split the Empire in two to make it more manageable. He selected the Eastern Empire for himself with Constantinople as its capital (today known as the Byzantine Empire) Maximiniano was given the Western Empire with its capital in Mediolanum (modern Milan). In 402 A.D. the capital was moved to Ravenna.

Ruling as an autocrat, Diocletian also created a new system of succession, consequently removing any semblance of republicanism in Rome. Roman rulers had preferred the system of adoption. The emperor adopted a son and made him his heir. The military preferred biological succession, father to son, while the senate assumed the right t elect their leader. Diocletian created what came to be known as the tetrarchy or the rule of four. With division of the Empire into West and East, each was ruled by an emperor and a pro-emperor. The two senior emperors, one in Rome and the other in Constantinople, took the name 'Augustus ' while the two subordinate emperors were called 'Caesar'. When each 'Augustus' died, each 'Caesar' replaced him as 'Augustus' and selected a 'Caesar' to replace himself.

(Diocletian had also attempted to build a new basis for imperial legitimacy and power through the pagan state religion with himself as a semi-divine monarch and high priest. Perhaps it was to preserve this legitimacy and power that as Emperor he issued severe edicts and cruel punishments including renunciation of the Catholic faith, torture or punishment by death.)

The Empire of the West existed intermittently between the third century and the fifth century after Diocletian's tetrarchy and the unifications associated with Constantine the Great.

Theodosius I was the last Roman emperor to rule over a unified Roman Empire. After his death in 395 A.D., the Roman Empire was permanently divided. It ended officially with the abdication of Romulus Augustus in 476 A.D. under pressure from Odoacer, the barbarian. (Odoacer was the first barbarian king of Italy. He assumed power in 476 A.D. which marks as the date of the fall of the Empire of the West. A German warrior, Odoacer worked his way up through the ranks of the Roman army. When the western emperor, Julius Nepos, was overthrown by the Roman general, Orestes, Odoacer defeated Orestes, deposed and exiled Romulus Augustus, and refused to acknowledge any new western emperor, declaring himself king of Italy.) Odoacer's greed for land and power spurred him onto new conquests in the North and East of Italy. Odoacer's expansionist trends fomented concern in the Byzantine Empire and also with Theodoric and his Ostrogoth leaders. In 489 A.D. Theodoric, king of the Ostrogoths invaded Italy and Odoacer was unable to stop his conquest. He surrendered the city of Ravenna in 493 A.D. and was killed as he attended a banquet hosted by Theodoric.

From 440 A.D. to 491 A.D., Germanic tribes, known as Vandals, made their "tour" of the Mediterranean, too. With a narrow base in the Andalusia area of the Iberian peninsula, the Vandals, in 428 A.D. with the cooperation of the disaffected Roman viceroy, launched an eleven year campaign leading to the capture and occupation of all provinces belonging to the Roman Empire in North Africa. Subsequent to the victories in North Africa, in 439 A.D. the Vandals led by Geiseric, invaded nearby Sicily. Roman forces occupying Sicily were no more effective in the defense of the island than those in Africa had been. Soon, the largest island in the Mediterranean was added to the Vandals growing empire.

Geiseric, realizing the force of his antagonist, Odoacer, in the North, shrewdly planned co-existence with his Italian neighbors to the North through a compromise over Sicily. The Vandals entered into a treaty in 476 A.D. with Odoacer under which they ceded Sicily to Odoacer but with an agreement that Odoacer would pay an annual tribute to Geiseric.

After Theodoric's conquest of Italy in 489 A.D., Sicily was next. In 491 A.D. he installed a Goth ruler on the island and the treaty agreement of tribute to the Vandals was relegated to the past. Ostrogoths ruled from 491 A.D. to 535 A.D. but their rule ended abruptly with the death of their leader, Theodorico. On the mainland and in Sicily, during his short reign, Teodorico, a firm admirer of Roman civilization, had hoped to join the two cultures in peaceful coexistence, but his politics of conciliation failed.

Teodorico was not the usual, uneducated barbarian chieftain; he had been educated in Constantinople and had received permission from the Byzantine Emperor, Zeno, to install himself in Italy as his deputy. His plan for peaceful coexistence failed and he turned to violence and punishment against his Christian and Roman opposition. After his death, Justinian, the new emperor of Byzantium, took advantage of the moment and sent his general, Belisarius, to destroy the Ostrogoths.

Justinian's aim was to restore the earlier Roman Empire around Byzantium (Constantinople) by reclaiming areas in the Mediterranean lost to Germanic tribes. In 527, Justinian[31] ascended the throne of Byzantium. In 535 A.D. his general, Belisario, defeated the Ostrogoths in a war that had spread ruin for 18 years. Cities and countryside were devastated and the population was decimated by pestilence and famine. One of Emperor Justinian's greatest contributions was his Justinian Code, the codification of Roman law. Under his legal advisor, Tribonian, the accumulation of 1,000 years of Roman legal material was gathered, unified, and edited. He failed in his repeated attempts to reconcile eastern and western theological differences and left a weakened empire, but his legacy was a magnificently rebuilt Hagia Sophia in Constantinople, the magnificent churches in Ravenna, and his Justinian Code of Roman law.

As the first step in his campaign to expel the Ostrogoths from Italy and regain the Italian peninsula for the eastern Roman(Byzantine) Empire, Emperor Justinian dispatched an army to invade Sicily in 535 A.D. The invading army, led by General Belisario found the Sicilian populace receptive in the expulsion of the Ostrogoths and swept through the island finding spirited resistance only in Palermo, but that was quickly overcome.

By 553 A.D., Italy and Sicily had become provinces of the Byzantine Empire and were governed by a Byzantine administrator whose headquarters were in Ravenna. (It was during this early period of Byzantine rule, that Ravenna's magnificent monuments, particularly San Vitale and Sant'Apollinare, were built.) There was an external appearance of tranquillity, but none of the desperately needed administrative, social, and commercial improvements were realized. Of little interest to the new administrator was the rest of Byzantium's conquered territory, including Sicily, and no assistance was given to rebuild a land destroyed by battles. In fact, the new administrator worsened the situation by imposing excessive taxation which impoverished the island.

As the Byzantines ruled, the Sicilians generally remained faithful to Roman orthodoxy. An attempt was made by Byzantium to draw the Sicilians away from Roman influence by confiscating the holdings of the Church and placing the ecclesiastic hierarchy under the rule of the patriarch of

Constantinople. During the two hundred years of Byzantine rule, the popes did their best to Romanize the Sicilian church. However, the need to maintain a viable relationship with the provincial Byzantine administration was acted upon, and bishops were instructed not to interfere in secular disputes. Although the pull for power between East and West was strong, a preference for the Greek language persisted, as did an affinity for eastern culture. With the Byzantine occupation of Sicily, the Greek language predominated again to the point that the educated and politically influential abandoned Latin and returned to Greek.[32]

The Byzantine Empire retained control of Sicily until the arrival of the Saracens (Muslims) almost three hundred years later.

The Arabs: Devastation / Recovery / Devastation

Soon after the death of Mohammad in 632 A.D., the rise of Islam and with it military consequences began to emerge. By 643 A.D. they had control of Syria and most of Egypt. By the end of the century, Saracens, as the followers of Islam were known) had expanded their conquests to include Persia and Armenia, and all of Northwest Africa. Even Constantinople was attacked in 673 and again in 717, but the attacks were repulsed.

From North Africa the Saracens seized Iberia (present day Spain and Portugal, where Roman rule had been replaced by Vandals and, finally, Visigoths.)

After minor raids into Sicily, the appeal of the terrestrial paradise was evident. Sicily not only was important strategically, but since the Byzantine conquest, it had become a main bulwark of eastern orthodoxy, another reason for Arab conquest. By 701 A.D. Arabs returned for third time to devastate the island. Finally in 827, an army of 10,000, Arabs, Berbers, and Spanish Muslims, landed in Mazzara, and total conquest of the island began.

Despite internal weakness and many enemies, Constantinople fought vigorously to defend its Byzantine Sicilian outpost against the Arab invasion. Consequently, the war dragged on for 50 years and lives and resources were destroyed and the island was tormented with famines and pestilence. The advance of the Arabs was slow but extremely ferocious as the most important cities were destroyed: Palermo and Messina in 831, Ragusa in 848, Syracuse in 878, and Taormina in 903. A.D. Slowly, a new civilization, one that was at its peak of power, was introduced to Sicily, and the island was torn away from Christianity and its Roman and Byzantine legacies.

The cataclysm of war ended. As peace returned to Sicily, Palermo was rebuilt and became the marvelous capital of the island, replacing Syracuse as the most important city in Sicily and, perhaps, in all Europe. Christianity submitted to Islam and the Greek language gave way to Arabic. In more than two centuries of occupation, the Arabs added their religion, literature, art, and science to the culture of the island. Writers of the period wrote of abundant springs and of an excellent system of irrigation. As the Greeks before them, it was their design to settle on the island as they arrived, probably in larger numbers than any other conqueror of the island before and after them.

Taxation continued to be excessive but was more intelligently administered, and those taxes which had been detrimental to agricultural development were removed. There was a healthy revival of commerce and handcrafts and an impressive enrichment of agriculture with Arab introduction of date and lemon trees, sugar cane, and cotton. Besides agriculture, the tuna industry prospered as a new and elaborate technique was introduced. Silver, lead, mercury, sulphur and mineral oils were produced. Sicilian salt became famous abroad. The art of manufacturing silk and textiles quickly played an important role in the economy of the island.[33] The Arabs divided Sicily into three administrative partitions, western, northeastern, and southeastern, overseen by *kadi* who, in turn, were governed by an *emir* who lived in Palermo. The capital had become a city of over 300,000 with thriving industries and commerce. The populace was divided into four distinct groups: the independents, the tributaries who paid taxes but were otherwise free, the vassals who were booty of war and were subjugated, and the serfs who slaved on large estates. A popular folk rhyme of the era recalls the Arab persecution of Christians:

C'è lu gaitu, e gran pena ni duna:
voli arrinunziu a la fidi cristiana!

"The Arab *gaitu* gives us great pain:
wanting us to renounce our Christian faith."[34]

Unfortunately, the Arab conquest of Sicily caused grave consequences to the island. By 880 A.D. civil war existed between -Arabs of Palermo and Berbers of Agrigento. These internal divisions were already occurring when a new wave of North Africans arrived, intending to divide the legendary wealth of the island among themselves, only to find Sicily already almost completely sacked. Profiting from internal discord among Arabs, the Sicilians revolted against their oppressors and succeeded in defeating them at Caltavuturo.[35] Eventually the Sicilian revolt was quelled. Between 938 A.D. and 940 A.D., battles raged among Arabs again in the southwestern part of the island inflicting further destruction.

Arab invasions and subsequent civil wars made deforestation necessary for new encampments; woodlands were destroyed and cultivated areas were burned. Further destruction of Sicilian forests occurred as Arabian ships crossed the sea carrying precious Sicilian hardwood needed in Africa for the ships which maintained Arab supremacy in the Mediterranean. By the 10th century the Tunisian dynasty was weakened, and Christian Europe finally was given the opportunity to counterattack against Muslim Sicily.[36]

Arab culture was assimilated into the eclectic character of the Sicilian and Sicily had become Muslim in many ways, but the end was soon to arrive. Arab control was slipping and, circa 1030 A.D., in order to control a rebellion, the Arabs entered into a treaty with Byzantium. In 1038, the Byzantine Empire launched a counter thrust under the leadership of George Maniace, its chief general, who landed near Messina with a large army which included several hundred Norman mercenaries. Maniace occupied the island for several years attempting to conquer it; the result was further destruction of the land. Assisted by discord among Saracens and strengthened by wide support among Sicilians, Byzantine forces captured Messina, then Syracuse. The recall of Maniace in 1042 and his replacement as leader caused an immediate turn in the fortunes of war. The Byzantine army was pushed back across the island. The Norman mercenaries were not long in returning, led by their leader, Roger de Hauteville, who was fighting at the time in southern Italy.

II: Moments of Glory

(Norsemen, later known as Normans, conquered Normandy in the 10th century A.D., and adopted Christianity and the customs and language of France. Norsemen were Scandinavian Vikings who raided and then settled the coasts of western Europe. With their arrival, France was threatened with a return to the barbarism from which it was just emerging (c.843). Norse settlements on the river banks were interfering with French commerce and navigation. In 911, King Charles II granted them the Duchy of Normandy, perhaps to contain and appease them. Early in the 11th century, bands of Normans, as the Norsemen came to be called, appeared in southern Italy where they first aided the local nobles in their rebellion against Byzantine rule. In 1059 Pope Nicholas II authorized these warriors, although not very Christian in their behavior, to control the territory of southern Italy, and in return the Normans agreed not to recognize the religious authority of Constantinople. As they fought to expel the Byzantines, the Normans proceeded to take over the land. The sons of Tancred de Hauteville led these expeditions. In 1059, Robert Guiscard, a son of Tancred, received from Pope Nicholas II the Duchies of Apulia, Calabria, and the island of Sicily, which was yet to be conquered. Another brother, Roger, eventually conquered Sicily.

Ruggero d'Altavilla (Roger de Hauteville) landed in Messina in 1061, and by 1091 had conquered all of Sicily. was given the title of Count of Sicily and Calabria. Pope Urban II also granted him the invaluable position of apostolic ambassador, which freed him from feudal submission to the Duchy of Puglia and gave him the power to nominate bishops in territory under his jurisdiction. This gave him absolute unity of power and set the stage for the first modern kingdom in an era in which most of Europe was still barbarian.

The island was Muslim territory when arrived, and, as he did not want to antagonize his non-Christian subjects, he was tolerant of Greek, Latin, and Arab traditions coexisting on the island. He respected the language and religion of his subjects while he directed the reorganization of Christian worship.[37]

He began a process of Latinization by introducing an altogether new ruling class. His Greek-Orthodox Sicilian subjects were not endowed with fiefs (landed estates or *latifondi*) nor elevated to the aristocracy. None of the chief *latifondisti* seems to have been native to the island. To fill positions of importance, first preferred Normans and Frenchmen, and then Lombards from the mainland, who were given land in return for military support.

Normans had great impact on Sicilian society, although theirs was not an *en masse* settlement such as the Arab's had been. By 1200 A.D., this mainly Arabic-speaking island had become largely Latinized in speech. The Normans recognized that Sicilians possessed a superior culture and administrative system, to which they quickly adapted, and to which they added their own efficiency and purpose, leading them to many exceptional achievements.[38]

After his death, Roger was first succeeded as Count of Sicily by his first son, who died three years later, followed by a second son, Roger.

Under his son, Ruggero II, Sicily had its Golden 50 years (1105-1154). Tall, dark haired, bearded and corpulent, he ruled his kingdom with diplomacy, ruthlessness, wisdom, and skill from his magnificent palace in Palermo. Many historians have termed his kingdom the best governed state in the Middle Ages. Ruggero II made the island one of the most perfect realms in Europe. He encouraged an eclectic harmony which united Arab and Christian colleagues from Sicily and the mainland. Pa-lermo, the capital, became a city of many splendors.[39] The island continued to absorb and assimilate. Soon the Norman conquerors were wearing satin, building harems, and writing poetry. Ethnic culture flourished alongside one another with ease as the island grew in prosperity.

Ruggero II was given the title of King of Sicily in 1129 during a session of parliament in Salerno where he convened not only nobles and ecclesiastics, but, anticipating more modern parliaments, he also had city and public officials present. He tightened and strengthened the internal administration of his kingdom, and he recruited a large army with which he conquered Tunisia, part of Lybia, Thebes, and Corinth by 1149. He occupied Corfù and Cephalonia.[40] Although he did not lead his troops personally as his father had done before him, he maintained complete control of his realm. He prevented his landed aristocracy (*latifondisti*) from gaining power through their feudal militia. Their authority was undermined by Ruggero's strong professional army which stood guard alongside the local militia. Furthermore, feudal justice was controlled by provincial judges travelling from city to city enforcing the King's law. Ruggero's laws were respected and local areas did not fall into the hands of the feudal aristocracy; private citizens did not find it necessary to take justice in their own hands as they would later.

Ruggero's government derived great wealth from the island and its people. Sicilian silk, salt, sulphur, and coral fishing industries were revitalized. Agriculture prospered. Sicilian warships sailed the Mediterranean and a merchant marine was developed which exacted payment of tribute from ships navigating in the area. 's income was among the greatest of the kings of Europe. The city of Palermo yielded more in income than his Norman cousins succeeded in extracting from all of England.[41]

In 1138, a meeting took place between and his distinguished guest from North Africa, the Arab geographer, Al-Idrisi. The agenda was the creation of the first accurate and scientific map of the entire known world. Al-Idrisi found a king who was born in Sicily, the son of a Norman soldier of fortune, educated by Greek and Arab tutors, living an oriental life style complete with harem and eunuchs, who was sometimes referred to as the baptized sultan of Sicily.

Although a few mariners' maps did exist, most of these remained in the hands of navigators. Colorful European maps showed a round earth composed of three continents equal in size: Asia, Africa, and Europe separated by a narrow band of water. What had in mind was something as factual as the mariners' charts, but that encompassed the entire known world. His purpose was to produce a work which would sum up all the contemporary knowledge of the physical world. To carry out the project, established an academy of geographers – 12 scholars. The scope of his plan was grand. wanted to know the exact condition of every area under his rule, and of the world outside, boundaries, climate, roads, rivers, and seas, and the coasts they bordered. The academy presented with a silver globe weighing 400 Kg. On it Al-Idrisi meticulously recorded the continents with trade routes, lakes and rivers, major cities and plains and mountains.

Ruggero II died in 1154, leaving his reign to his son, Guglielmo. Sicily remained prosperous, but increased opposition by *latifondisti* caused great unrest. The emperors of the East and West and the Papacy prepared to exploit the displeasure of the island's feudal aristocracy which was impatient for more power. Sicily did not have the resources to defend itself against betrayal from within and the intrigues of both the Pope and Byzantium. The *latifondisti*, as their economic and social power increased, resented the political power that their benefactor, Ruggero II, held over them. They coveted his control of the judiciary, the government, and the army. The *latifondisti* also resented his suppression of any opposition on their part by exile and confiscation of property. The more ambitious *latifondisti* took advantage of Guglielmo's weaker and less efficient reign to start changing the internal balance of power. Because internal strife weakened his realm, he came to be called Guglielmo il Malo (William the Bad).[42]

His son, Guglielmo II, also faced grave situations, but he fared better than his father had, and he became Guglielmo il Buono (William the Good). He supported Pope Alexander III in his antiSwabian politics, even sending aid to the Lombard communes in their effort to defeat Frederick Barbarossa. The Sicilian King's international position had become so powerful that he married Giovanna of England, daughter of Henry II, after refusing the hand of a Byzantine Princess, daughter of Emperor Comneno. During his participation in the third crusade in 1189, as he prepared new weapons for the reconquest of Jerusalem, he died. As king, Guglielmo II welcomed artists and soldiers of fortune of all races and religions to his court; he enriched Sicily with the magnificent Cathedral of Palermo, the Cloister and the Benedictine Abbey at Monreale, and the opulent Arabian-style palaces called Cuba and Zisa; unfortunately, too much of the island's wealth was dissipated. While the maritime communes of the Italian peninsula were beginning to amass great wealth, Sicilian commerce was stagnating. Political opposition was emerging from Messina and Palermo, and resentment grew at the lack of autonomous municipal governments. Guglielmo II made a political error of grave consequences. Accepting the advice of the English archbishop of Palermo, Walter Offamil, he permitted the marriage of his aunt Costanza d'Altavilla, heiress to the Sicilian throne, to the Swabian Henry VI, son of Frederick Barbarossa.[43]

Norman England and Sicily had close ties during this period of turmoil. Richard Palmer, friend of Thomas Becket, became Archbishop of Syracuse; Walter Offamil and his brother, Bartholomew, both became Archbishops of Palermo. Not only were they very supportive of the *latifondisti*, they also advanced the spread of Christianity on the island and furthered the subordination of Greek to Latin culture on the island.

In 1190, after the death of Guglielmo II, Parliament elected Tancredi d'Altavilla king of Sicily with the enthusiastic support of the populace. His reign was difficult as he had to battle the barons of Puglia who called in Henry I of Germany for support. battled the Muslims who were in a state of rebellion on the island; he faced Richard the Lion-Hearted who wanted restitution of his sister Giovanna's dowry now that she was widowed by the death of Gu-glielmo II. He fought well and was successful until Henry I, who had assumed the title, Henry VI of Sicily, following his marriage to Costanza of Sicily, allied himself with the republics of Genoa, Pisa, and Venice. Still kept Henry VI away from the island until his death in 1194. Then his kingdom went to his young son, Guglielmo III. The barons of

Puglia summoned Henry VI again and with the support of the fleets of Pisa and Genova he occupied Catania and Syracuse. The Altavilla dynasty was concluded with the imprisonment of young Guglielmo III in a German prison where he died in 1199, after being horribly mutilated.[44]

The Swabians : Lust For The Island's Wealth

The death of a childless Gulglielmo II and the marriage of his Aunt , daughter of Ruggero II, heiress to the throne subsequently led to the conquest of the island by Henry, son of Frederick I, King of the Swabians and Emperor of the Holy Roman Empire's husband ruled Germany as Henry I, and Sicily as Henry VI. Henry looked to Sicily's wealth as support for his territorial ambitions in southern Europe and the Mediterranean. The conquest of Sicily had long been coveted by the emperors of the Holy Roman Empire, and the marriage of supplied the pretext for conquest, just as the alliance with the naval powers of Genoa and Pisa supplied the means. In 1194 Henry was crowned Henry VI, King of Sicily.

Upon entering Palermo, Henry saw a land of conquest to be exploited to the bone, and he and his followers filled their coffers with gold, priceless gems, and silks. He did nothing to placate his subjects, and used the island only for its wealth. His German generals and Cavaliers of the Teutonic Order were given large tracts of land (*latifondi*), including the vast landholdings confiscated from the clergy. , his wife, was powerless to stop the torture and anguish of her people during his horrendous reign. The populace revolted and Henry VI took dreadful vendettas on his adversaries; women, clergy, and countless others who had no hand in the protests were also killed, as he vainly attempted to end the insurrections. His poor health forced him to retire to Messina[45] where he died in 1197 at the age of 32 years. He left his kingdom of Sicily to his young son Federico II.

The Holy Roman Empire of the West survived for more than 1000 years after that day in 800 A.D. when Pope Leo III placed a crown on the head of Charlemagne as he named him Charles Augustus, Emperor of the Romans. The development of the Holy Roman Empire can be traced from the time of Charlemagne, when people saw the Empire as the continuation of the Roman Empire of Augustus, through the rule of the Ottonian emperors – with almost continuous conflicts between popes and Emperors and eventually through the rise and eventual decline of the Hapsburgs. In its 1000 year existence it was beset from within and from without by political, religious, and social turmoil. Occasionally it appeared that peace was within reach, as when the sons of Charlemagne agreed to a division of his lands and again, later, when Emperor Otto III, grandson of Charlemagne, foreseeing imminent danger took very bold steps as they became necessary. When the Princes of Poland, Moravia, Bohemia, and Hungary, who were on the verge of becoming Christians, faced the prospect of forceful takeover by the Germanic church whose intention it was to evangelize and penetrate politically, they recoiled in alarm and looked to Rome and Byzantium for Allies. Emperor Otto III in the year 999 set out to 'win' the allegiance of these territories which the Empire was at risk of losing to Rome or Byzantium. He, as Emperor of the Holy Roman Empire, set up a Polish Archbishopric at Gnesen in Cracow, Kolberg, and Breslau. Otto placed the golden circlet upon the Polish leader's' brow, honored him with the title of 'Friend and Confederate of the Roman People' and 'Co worker of the Empire' and patricius. The Emperor returned the tribute that the Polish leader had been forced to pay. It was Otto's intention that Poland, Hungary, and other lands should become confederate states of varying status similar to those that had surrounded the old Roman Empire. The Emperor was hegemon, had rights of leadership, but this Empire was to act as an umbrella organization, uniting in the loosest way possible ethnic groups of varying size and holding them together by the most diverse of ties. The Empire came close to becoming one grand union of peoples joined in a federation of states which encompassed widely diverse societies of populations with widely differing cultures.

Hungary, encouraged by the generosity of Otto III at Gnesen, Poland, opted, at once, for the West, for the Latin Church, and Latin civilization. With Otto's help, Stephen converted his country to Christianity, Stephen I received a king's crown from Otto, and Otto had successfully demonstrated to the Poles and Hungarians that it was possible to attach oneself to western civilization, Latin culture, and the Latin Church, become friend to the Emperor without having to become German. Prior to this decisive moment, the Byzantine Church had hoped to press through Hungary and conclude with the re-conquest of Europe as Justinian had intended to accomplish from Ravenna, (west coast of Italy) considered the sacred citadel.

Unfortunately, before long, competition began to grow between the papacy and the Emperor.

Otto III intended that he would reign from Rome as the 'servant of the Apostles, therefore putting himself on an equal footing with the Byzantine 'isapostolos', (the apostle) the new Constantine, the new Justinian.. Otto saw himself as St. Peter's deputy.

The Salian emperors (1024 – 1125 came of Frankish stock and were descended from the Ottonian dynasty and became the forbears of the Hohenstaufen. Under Emperor Conrad II Rome became the imperial city, the city of the 'King of the Romans'. He was ruthless in dealing with bishops who opposed him on political grounds, banishing or imprisoning them.

With Emperor Henry III (1039–56) imperial power reached its zenith which resulted in a determined Pope Leo IX fighting to uphold what he conceived to be his papal rights. He gathered around him in Rome a group of collaborators and the monastic reform movement, the group which also included Hildebrand, who later became the determined Pope Gregory VII. The collision would cause monumental struggles in the future. Pope Gregory VII would become the revolutionary voice of the 11th century calling for freedom of the church, freedom from control, from 'overlordship' exercised by worldly rulers and the clergy they controlled. It was Gregory's plan to build a league of European peoples in the form of one great European system of vassalage in which individual countries would be tied to St. Peter by legal and political ties. Many countries submitted including Hungary in 1074 and Russia in 1075. Aim was unification of all Christian peoples and suppression of heretics. To strengthen the Church further he advocated celibacy for members of the clergy admonishing the worldly entanglements and loyalties of married priests. The struggle of papal investiture gained impetus in the late 11th century. There had been no general agreement as to the power of popes and Holy Roman emperors in installing German bishops. It was generally recognized that both had rights in the matter. Lay investitures was the term used for investitures of clerics by the king or emperor.

Pope Gregory VII and the Holy Roman Emperor, Henry IV began the struggle. The clerical reform movement generated the crisis; it was necessary that the church have the power of selecting bishops and that lay investitures be abolished if reforms were to be carried out. In 1075 Pope Gregory forbade lay investiture and contention began earnestly. Subsequent popes condemned lay investiture, but not until 1122 did churchmen succeed in bringing about an agreement in the Concordat of Worms between Henry V and Pope Calixtus II.

The intensifying struggle between Pope and Emperor had to end with the latter's position reduced to 'German king, a king like any other. Pope Gregory excommunicated Henry IV, who, in the end marched on Rome, deposed Gregory VII, appointed the archbishop of Ravenna as pope and had himself crowned emperor by the new pope, Clement II.]

(It is perhaps necessary to clarify the position of the above-mentioned Frederick I, Emperor of the Holy Roman Empire, and father of Henry VI of Sicily. With the fall of the Roman Empire and the known world eventually divided roughly into three parts: the Byzantine Empire of the East, the Roman Papacy, and the Holy Roman Empire (which

pretended to champion Christianity. The existence of papal power conflicted with imperial power and although the Concordat of Worms, in 1122, decreed the separation of church and state, rivalry between popes and emperors worsened.

In fact, in the 13th century, the hostilities between the two rival groups intensified while newly established political and military forces (the communes in Italy and the three first large monarchies of Europe - France, Spain, and England) entered the conflict. After achieving papal investitures, the church's powers were greatly strengthened and members of the church obeyed only the laws of the church and not the law of the land they inhabited. Ecclesiastical power grew and its sphere of influence strengthened so, during the 12th century that the Emperor was vastly undermined.

In 1152 a decisive turn of events occurred in Germany with the election of Frederick I, known as Barbarossa, King of the Swabians. Related to the dynasties in conflict (the Hohenstaufen and the Welfs), he was acclaimed by both sides as the Prince of Peace. Having settled the rivalry between the two ruling dynasties, he determined to restore imperial authority on the Italian communes[46] that had become mostly autonomous.

In 1154 Federico Barbarossa arrived in Italy, destroyed and burned several northern cities and headed towards Rome. The Pope had been unseated and Rome was governed as a commune by Arnaldo of Brescia, an opponent of the temporal power of the Church. Barbarossa captured Arnaldo and turned him over to Pope Adrian in exchange for the imperial crown. Only with the imperial crown placed on his head by the Pope in Rome could Barbarossa strengthen his authority over all of Christian Europe. As Emperor he marched through Italy six times attempting to conquer, and only in 1176, at Legnano, did the League of Free Italian Cities, sustained by the Pope, defeat him. For the first time, the people in the communes of Italy succeeded in opposing the Holy Roman Empire. Despite his defeat in the North, as a result of the marriage of his son, Henry, to of Sicily, the "Imperial Eagle" of the Swabians would fly over Sicily as Henry VI ruled.)[47]

Federico Barbarossa responded quickly to Pope Gregory VIII's summons to all European kings to enlist support for the 3rd crusade and departed quickly with 100,000 men in 1189. After a series of difficulties during the journey, he died by drowning in Armenia, and his army disintegrated. (The Holy Roman Empire / Friedrich Heer / Frederick A. Praeger / Publisher / New York / 1967)

When the reign of Henry VI ended with his death in 1197, his three year old son, Federico II, became his heir. Henry VI had tried to make a German of his son, but Constanza of Altavilla, born and brought up in Palermo, raised her son as a Norman-Sicilian in spite of grave disapproval of the German landbarons. hoped to recapture the spirit of tolerance, which had been so beneficial to Sicily during the reign of her father, Ruggero II, and combine it with the best of the present to create a propitious future for the realm. After her husband's death, allied herself with the Pope. As the relationship improved, she assumed the position of "favorite daughter" of the Church, and, with the Pope's blessing, the very young Federico II was crowned king, in 1198, in the Duomo of Palermo. With 's death in the same year, Pope Innocent III became the regent of the Kingdom of Sicily and tutor to the young king.

Despite the papal regency, a period of anarchy followed. A series of battles and intrigues brought destruction and ruin for the people and the land. A group of Swabian *latifondisti*, enriched by grants from Henry VI, overcame Papal troops and took possession of Palermo and the young King. In addition, the Arabic- speaking Moslems, who had been persecuted and driven into the interior during Henry's reign, reacted quickly to the anarchy of Henry's death with riots. Many had lost their means of livelihood, some had left the island, and many took advantage of this state of civil war by banding together, stealing food, and trying to recover lost property. Like many subsequent "bandits" in Sicilian history, they were exploited, in this case, by the German *latifondisti* who could only gain by the chaos and rebellion.[48]

Federico II: The Eclectic Sicilian School

As Federico II grew, his education came from a variety of tutors and sources. The crossroads of cultures of his environment became the foundation of his education and endlessly nourished his innate intelligence and curiosity. This grandson of Ruggero II and Frederick Barbarossa, ruling with absolute authority, united three cultures —Moslem, Latin-Germanic, and Sicilian-Norman — in peaceful coexistence on the island. He did, however, find it necessary to forcefully exile tens of thousands of rebellious Moslems to Lucera.

Federico spoke six languages including Arabic. He had friendships with members of Islamic royalty and he kept a harem in Sicily. He was schooled in Arabic philosophy and mathematics. Ahead of his time, he democratically effected the inclusion to parliament of city representatives from Palermo, Messina, Catania, Syracuse, Trapani and many other Sicilian cities in 1240, foreshadowing the House of Commons. (In England it was not until 1264 that city representatives were admitted to parliament.).

Sicilian culture reached exceptional splendor. Federico II, a man of unusual intellect, gifted with remarkable aesthetic sensitivity, surrounded himself with the greatest minds of his age, and because of him Sicilian culture spread to the continent. Federico II earned for himself the title, 'Stupor Mundi' – 'Marvel of the World'.

In 1220 Federico II was crowned Emperor of the Holy Roman Empire by Pope Honorius. In 1225 he married the daughter and heiress of John Brienne, the King of Jerusalem. After the death of Pope Honorius, Pope Gregory IX ordered Emperor Federico II to begin his crusade to the Holy Land. The Emperor obeyed without delay but returned to Sicily quickly, claiming illness. As intrigue of court and papacy would have it, Federico II, once the favorite of the papacy, was excommunicated in 1228 by the newly elected pope for his hasty return and for his efforts against the Templars and other loyal Catholics. Federico set off again in 1228 though, ironically, he did so, as an excommunicated leader. He organized the sixth crusade and, upon entering Jerusalem in 1228, crowned himself emperor of the Holy Roman Empire in the Church of the Holy Sepulcher.

He claimed the crown of Jerusalem for himself through his wife, heiress of the throne.

Battles against the papacy for survival of the Empire and against Italian communes and German barons plagued Federico II during his long reign in Sicily. He was surrounded by disloyalty and conspiracies. Perhaps, the most disturbing was the rebellion led against him by his own son, Henry, who from early youth had been educated as a German in Germany and had been crowned king of Germany by Federico II, himself, years earlier. Henry had joined the Lombards in their revolts of 1234. Dreadful battles were fought by troops of the Holy Roman Empire to regain and retain control of power in northern Italy where the Lombard League fought for its existence but was finally overcome by Federico's forces aided by mercenaries from Hungary, Germany, and Provence. Henry remained his father's prisoner until his death in 1242.[50]

In 1245 at the Council of Lyon the emperor was once again condemned and expelled from the Church as a heretic and deposed as an emperor. Federico II died in Apulia in the southeast of the mainland. As emperor he had chosen Jusinian as his sacral prototype. He meant men to revere his state as an 'empirial church' in which he was the high priest.

During the reign of Emperor Federico II, Sicily became an extraordinary land ahead of its time and one of the most significant precursors of the *Rinascimento*. The famous Sicilian School contributed much to the growth of literature in the vernacular on the mainland. The poetry of Ciullo d'Alcamo and Guido da Lentini in Sicilian vernacular was acclaimed by Dante and Petrarca. They acknowledged the preeminence of these Sicilian poets and the importance of this first Italian literary language. To Jacopo da Lentini is attributed the invention of basic lyric forms such as the sonnet. (Petrarca later brought fame to this new poetic form in *Il Canzoniere* which represents, among other things, the story of his love for Laura). Although his court became a creative center for literature, Federico II did not neglect other arts and the sciences. The sculptors, Bartolomeo and Nicola, the artist, Tommaso Schifani, and the architect, Riccardo da Lentini, all made notable contributions at Federico's court. Leonardo Fibonacci of Pisa, and Giovanni da Palermo, two of the most important mathematicians of the Middle Ages, Michele Scotto, the astrologist, and Piero della Vigna, the poet from Capua, made contributions too. Senators, orators, poet-musicians, jousters, and fencing masters from all parts of the island and the mainland were invited to Palermo, the center of creativity.[49]

Federico II is credited, together with Pier della Vigna, with the adaptation of the principals of Roman law into a Medieval Code which replaced old feudal laws. His eclectic interests led to the improvement of the sugar and silk industries. He also turned his attention to improving methods of irrigation.

The destruction of the Holy Roman Empire received its final thrust after Federico's death as Pope Innocent IV (1243-1254) vowed to destroy this "race of vipers". The Pope had no intention of allowing the Papal States to be hemmed in from north and south by Norman-Swabian domination. Although he died of intestinal fever in Puglia on the mainland, Federico II, by testamentary disposition, was buried in the duomo in Palermo next to the tombs of his parents and his grandfather, Ruggero II. After his death, the Pope energetically averted the succession to the throne by any of Federico 's sons. His design to exterminate the sons and heirs of Federico II was accomplished through the French. The French Pope, Urban IV (1261-4) brought in Charles Anjou, brother of King Louis IX to campaign against the heirs to the empire One by one the sons were killed on the battlefield by the papal army. Federico's son, Manfredi, 16 years of age, continued the fight against the papal army and gained control of and ruled parts of northern Italy and the Kingdom of the Two Sicilies. Parliament elected Manfredi King of Sicily despite his papal excommunication in 1254. Manfredi was finally killed in 1266 in Benevento on the mainland in a battle fought against Charles d'Anjou, who had been offered the crown of Sicily by Pope Clemente IV. Papal politics had turned to fomenting anti-Norman-Swabian sentiment in Sicilian cities. The news of popular uprisings, convincingly presented to Louis IX of France by papal emissary, convinced him to accept the crown of Sicily for his brother, Charles d'Anjou. A final heir, Corradino, a grandson of Federico, was decapitated by Charles d'Anjou in the market square in Naples, in 1268. Federico's son, Enzo, held prisoner for many years in a prison in Bologna, died in 1272, leaving a legacy of beautiful poems. The papacy had triumphed over the Empire of the Hohenstaufen.

From 1250 – 1273 the Holy Roman Empire was engulfed in the interregnum. Where was the Empire? Territories were lost as subsequent emperors selected different sites as capital of the Empire. With Rudolph of Hapsburg's election as King in 1273 he quickly set out to reclaim those territories lost during the interregnum.

Federico II's Holy Roman Empire died with him. His legacy was his great success in promoting the unity of Sicily's multi-cultured potential. Unfortunately, as grand as his accomplishments were, Federico's absolute authority was greatly detrimental to the future of the island. When Federico II took over the reign of the island, he affirmed his rule with such vengeance that he suppressed all signs of independence, anarchy, and rebellion in the land. Sicily was still sufficiently wealthy that its cities could have flourished, but nothing similar to the flourishing of the independent communes of the mainland was allowed to occur on the island. His authority was too powerful and the tribute he exacted was too excessive to allow cities the local independence and monetary resources needed for progress. Each city was dominated by a fortress whose troops controlled the area. Any privileges previously enjoyed by the cities were annulled if they were incompatible with his idea of command. The rebellion this caused in Messina was mercilessly crushed by Federico's army. The submission of the cities assured Federico that neither a class of merchants nor a class of public administrators would become independent and powerful enough to counterbalance his *latifondisti*. This void along with excessive taxation shaped the political, cultural, and economic decline of Sicily. Whenever a central government was missing or incompetent, it was the *latifondisti* and not the local municipalities who filled the void.[51]

The French: The Island Violated

As the Holy Roman Empire and its control in Sicily came to an end, central authority decayed, and the economy on the island deteriorated. After 1250, attempts were made by some cities to affirm themselves as communes as their northern counterparts, on the mainland, had done. These cities had been so weakened by their previous master, however, that all efforts eventually failed. Lack of central power led many to ignore the law and resort to private justice. At this critical moment, as feudalism was declining in the rest of Europe, the French arrived on the island. A power struggle was raging between the *latifondisti* who were exploiting the void in central government, and the weakened municipalities who were struggling to strengthen their control.[52]

It was in 1265 that Charles d'Anjou, brother of King Louis IX of France, landed in Sicily with his army to take the throne from King Manfredi who had held it since 1258. The result was a brutalized island. Manfredi could have become the popular hero, the defender of Sicilian independence against the Pope and the French. That all ended, however, with his death during the battle of Benevento on the mainland, fought against the French in 1266.

Progress and enlightenment ended as Charles d'Anjou destroyed the modern state created under the rule of his enemy and rival, Emperor Federico II. Since the French conquest was closely allied with the papacy and was, in part, a punitive crusade by the papacy, the advancing army had no obligation to respect person, property, or tradition. As the land was conquered and sacked, the new king of Sicily, Charles d'Anjou, enriched himself and his nobles with money and land through rapacious laws enforced with such oppression that the people were soon provoked into action. Archives attest to excessive taxation and, even worse, to the arbitrary and violent methods of tax collectors and soldiers whose actions were encouraged by their king. Peasants were forced to pay all taxes on projected annual income in advance. Failure to pay resulted in grave punishment.[53] The French forced payment of ransom on Sicilian *latifondisti* in return for the uncertain retention of their lands. Accusations were often invented by the new rulers, to justify the confiscation of these lands which were often given to French aristocrats who, frequently, turned the lands over to their families or soldiers.

The new king's imperialistic ambitions included Byzantium. Ironically,

Emperor Michael of Byzantium looked to Pope Gregory X for assistance against the schemes of Charles d'Anjou. Michael offered to end the schism between the Churches of East and West by embracing the dogma of the Trinity which was basic to the Roman Church. Pope Gregory agreed to Emperor Michael's proposal and kept Charles from Byzantium. The Greeks, however, refused the Trinity, and Pope Gregory lost hope for a union with the Eastern Church. Charles d'Anjou also felt threatened by his enemy, Peter of Aragon, to whom Byzantium had turned for support. The death of Pope Gregory enabled King Charles to force the election of the Frenchman, Martin IV, who, as pope, allowed Charles freedom to prepare an army for war against Byzantium.[54]

These new masters abused power, confiscated property, imprisoned their subjects and condemned them unjustly to cruel punishment and death. The island was governed badly; native Sicilians were often raped and murdered. The land was ripe for rebellion. In 1281, Sicilians sent a delegation which included the bishop of Patti and Fra Giovanni Marini, a Dominican, to Rome to the newly elected French pope, Martin IV. In the presence of the pope and of Charles d'Anjou, the new king of Sicily, they discussed the unbearable situation in their land. Once they emerged from their audience, they were arrested and imprisoned. The bishop escaped, but the Dominican remained until his death.

The insurrection of 1282, known as the Sicilian Vespers, erupted in front of the Church of the Holy Spirit near Palermo, on Easter Monday, at the start of vespers. One interpretation emphasizes the conspiracy between King Peter of Aragon and the Byzantine Emperor Michael Palaeologus to foment a revolt on the island against the French oppressors. The second interpretation involved a French sergeant and a Sicilian woman. Traditionally on the Tuesday after Easter, the citizens of Palermo traveled a short distance outside the city to Santo Spirito, to attend church and have supper. They would raise their tents, improvise taverns, eat, dance and sing, briefly forgetting their plight. A large patrol of French soldiers was present, one of whom eyed a young woman as she entered church on the arm of her husband. He ran to search her and on the pretext that she was concealing weapons, began fondling her. A Sicilian youth, angered by the insult, stabbed the Frenchman and killed him, while shouting, "Death to the French!" It was the signal for an immediate and tremendous rebellion. With stones, sticks, and weapons taken from the soldiers, the Sicilians killed them all.

That same night Palermo was proclaimed a commune and Sicilian leaders were elected. Rebellion led to revolution throughout the island. Extermination of the hated French was the consequence of eighteen years of Sicilian martyrdom. Only those Frenchmen who had not been cruel were spared. The resulting struggle to achieve liberty and justice explains why such a massacre has been looked upon as a glorious moment of Sicilian history. A parliament was convened and the city of Palermo was declared an independent republic. Cities and towns supported the new Republic by sending delegates to Palermo to begin creation of a confederation of independent communes. Support also came from some Sicilian *latifondisti*. [55]

The rebellion took several directions; first it rid the island of the oppressor; then it aimed to create a confederation of communes; finally, disastrously, it developed into a feudal revolt by the landed aristocracy against the formation of a strong central government. The Swabian *latifondisti*, still in Sicily after the defeat of the Holy Roman Empire, mobilized by the turn of events, plotted to take command of the situation before it took a direction undesirable to their ambitions. Their intrigues brought the defeat of centralized rule and the victory of feudal aristocracy a little closer.

An ominous change had been occurring among the *latifondisti* whose power had grown by dint of concessions, privileges, and money given by incumbent kings in return for service and loyalty. The problem perpetuated itself through Sicily's long history of foreign rule. The conflict extended into a power struggle between the older Sicilian *latifondisti* who were fighting to regain their land and power from foreigners who, by royal decree, had received vast tracts of land in Sicily. With the French presence on the island, replacement of many Sicilian *latifondisti* by Frenchmen left chaos among dispossessed Sicilian aristocrats. Some went into exile and lived in Spain where they sought protection and assistance at the Spanish court of Aragon. In return they pledged loyalty to Peter of Aragon as he planned the conquest of Sicily.

During that period after the Vespers, from April through August, as Sicilian patriots struggled to create a confederation of Sicilian communes, intrigue from Aragon and the constant threat of counter-attack from Charles d'Anjou and his French army tightened the noose on Sicily's fledgling and heroic attempt at independence. Patriotic conviction was forced to yield to reality.

The courageous attempt to be free from French oppression was part of a larger conflict in which the Spaniard, Peter of Aragon, and the Neapolitans were using the Sicilian *latifondisti* exiled in Spain in a plot to overcome the political power of the French. The Byzantine Michael VIII, motivated by his desire to end Charles d'Anjou's threat against Byzantium, also encouraged the revolt and fueled its rapid spread.[56]

The French army attempted to storm the city of Messina and regain control, but King Charles failed to conquer the will of the people. The French pope aided him by inhibiting Christian support of the rebellion. He admonished the populace to surrender to French domination or face excommunication. Charles d'Anjou organized an army of French, Guelphs from Lombardy and Tuscany, and Saracens, and with the aid of Venetian and Genoese ships and French armaments he had prepared for the battle against Byzantium, attacked Messina where he was finally defeated by the heroism of the Sicilian leaders, soldiers, and citizens including women, who aided and encouraged their men to fight on.[57]

The first leaders of the Sicilian revolt had not asked any outside nation for aid. The web of intrigues, by Michael of Byzantium, by Sicilian and Swabian *latifondisti*, and the French — prepared the groundwork for the Spanish presence on the island. The eventual arrival of military support from Spain came as a result of multiple intrigues and Sicily's desperate need for outside strength to end the lengthy French siege of Messina. Peter of Aragon went into action after he learned that the French Navy had been damaged. On the 30th of August, 1282, he landed at Trapani and on the 4th of September he entered Palermo amidst applause from the public. Troops, arms, food, and horses were supplied to the weary Sicilians, and the French were forced to retreat from their siege of Messina and flee the island.

The Sicilian Vespers purged the island of the French but it also resulted in the island's isolation from the mainland of Italy. This unpropitious consequence came into effect after the painful and corrosive "ninety-years war," from 1282 to1372, which bloodied and further destroyed the island; war between the French d'Anjou, the old master, and the Spanish Aragonese, newly arrived in Sicily, raged, and peace was not signed until 1372 at Avignon.

The Spaniards: Centuries of Eclipse

Peter III of Aragon laid claim to the throne of Sicily through his wife, daughter of Manfredi and grandaughter of Federico II. The Sicilian Parliament had exacted a pledge from Peter III to guarantee their Constitution and to assist Sicily in its fight for liberation from the French in return for Sicilian loyalty to him as their king. This was the beginning of the "ninety-years war" which bloodied the island from 1282 to 1372, as the French d'Anjou of Naples battled with the Spanish Aragonese for sovereignty of the island. When, in 1285, Peter of Aragon died, his son, Giacomo, was elected Sicily's new king. For this act of independence, all Sicilians were excommunicated by Pope Onorio IV for defying his demand that they yield to the French. Unfortunately, although Sicilians pledged loyalty to their new king, Giacomo, he plotted to return Sicily to the French. By yielding to the French, Giacomo hoped to gain favor with the Pope from whom he wanted confirmation of his succession to the throne of Spain after the death of his brother, Alfonso III. A pact was made with the Pope and Charles d'Anjou to turn Sicily over to Charles after Giacomo married Bianca d'Anjou and received his dowry from his French co-plotters. Sicilian loyalty was with their king as long as he was faithful to them, but when King Giacomo's treachery was exposed, they assembled Parliament, ended his term as king, and proclaimed his younger brother, the viceroy Federico, king, in 1296. A statute extracted while Federico was viceroy guaranteed liberty to the Sicilians, the convening of Parliament once a year, and the freedom to deliberate on the declaration of war. Sicilians hailed Federico III enthusiastically as their sovereign. They fought valiantly at his side against assaults from the French, the Guelphs of Italy, the Spaniards, and the Papal States in their pronouncements of excommunication, as they attempted to hold on to their independence. Federico III became the strenuous defender of Sicilian right to independence. He increased the power of parliament, improved the social welfare of the downtrodden, and set up a state- organized school in Sicily. He battled heroically together with his loyal subjects against the French and the pope for decades until, grieved and disillusioned, he died in 1337. Upon his tomb is inscribed the couplet:

Sicaniae populi macrent; coelestia gaudent
numina; terra gemit: rex Fridericus obiit.

"The people of Sicily cry; the angels of heaven rejoice;
Earth mourns: King Federico III is dead"[58]

With his death, a Spanish feudal state was firmly established on the island. After 1350, a general disintegration of society occurred. Rivalry between the Sicilian aristocracy and the newly created Spanish *latifondisti,* aggravated by the continuous larger rivalry between the French and the Spaniards, reached warlike proportions. Sicilian landbarons, betrayed by Spanish rulers on their own island, began to offer their allegiance to the French who cajoled them for support. The principal fracture occurred between two families, the Chiaramontes and the Alagonas, who had acquired vast tracks of land when French landholdings were confiscated after 1282. The Chiaramontes offered their loyalty to the French, whose army, aided by Neapolitan and German troops, landed on the island many times and completely devastated the territory along the southern coastline. They set fire to forests, destroyed trees and vineyards, prevented tuna fishing, killed agriculture and thus stopped commerce. Their adversaries remained loyal to their Spanish sovereign, hailing themselves the heroes of Sicilian independence, and extended their control over the northern part of the island, starving the inhabitants of entire areas into submission. Sheer exhaustion finally brought the "ninety-years' war" to an end in 1372.

By the final phase of the "ninety years war," feudal anarchy had torn Sicily apart, especially during the reign of Federico IV (1355-1377). He favored the almost total re-conquest of Sicily by the French d'Anjou, but in May of 1357 Sicilians were victorious in a sea battle off Catania which overturned the military situation; the war continued uneventfully until the peace at Avignon was signed in 1372 which underscored the definitive separation of Sicily from Naples, a division that was to last until 1860.

The historian, Antonino DiStefano speaks of "the heroic conscience" of the Sicilians, "willing to accept sacrifices, willing to dare the pope and his excommunications, willing to dare the powerful kings of Naples, France, and even the king of Aragon, who had been Sicily's sovereign," as the most beautiful page in the long and varied history of Sicily. "It is the people's voice in defense of its liberty, its law, and its sovereignty, written, not by foreign rulers or ministers, but by Sicilians, themselves."[60]

Spanish domination had a tragic effect on Sicily. Deprived already of contact with the East and North Africa, the island was parted from the mainland at the moment when Italy was entering its golden period of Petrarca, Dante, and the *Rinascimento.* For the next four hundred years Sicily was influenced, not by Italy during its period of glory, but by feudal Spain."

Memories of Federico II's splendid Sicilian civilization and of one of Europe's most perfect realms faded rapidly to the inner recess of the collective mind as this despoiled and spent populace faced another deplorable domination. Not only did the Spaniards fail to sustain and guide the people in their need to emerge from a turbulent and chaotic period, they encouraged violence and confiscated the lands of those Sicilian aristocrats who had aided the Spanish arrival on the island; they estranged the people and they further destroyed an already weakened middle class which would have strengthened the authority of the realm by maintaining domestic peace.

The power of Sicily's Parliament was weakened and declined. Its representatives deserted the assemblies, preferring representation by delegates. Sicilians were prevented from holding important offices which were given to the Spaniards by their king. Despotic rule, taxation, and impositions without representation angered the populace.

As years passed, Spanish rulers continued to distribute large land tracts to their Spanish compatriots, made many powerful concessions to these new *latifondisti,* and continued to weaken the authority of the central government with deepening disorganization and fragmentation. Under the self-serving totalitarian control of the Spaniards and the internal strife between the old and new landed aristocracy, the way was paved for further tragedy for Sicily.

Latifondisti, many of them Spaniards with no allegiance to Sicily, freed themselves from any control wherever possible, becoming most powerful, owning and controlling 2/3 of the land. They lived in castles high in the impregnable rocks, elected their captains and their own judges and thus became the law. The people were forced into submission, dependence, and obedience. The protective safeguards of Federico II's Constitution were now only a memory. In reality, the *latifondisti* ruled their immediate domains controlling the land, the mills, the ovens, and the tolls. This new enemy, this parasite from within, together with Spanish usurpation of liberty, further destroyed the human condition of the Sicilians.[61]

At the end of the 14th century, Sicilians succeeded in having their Parliament reconvened. A petition was presented requesting that fewer Spaniards be nominated to government positions and that only Sicilian laws be applied to Sicily. It also was proposed that members of Parliament be represented in the royal council and that, in case of the Spanish king's absence, some executive power be bestowed upon them. The attempt was to bring the Sicilian parliament closer to the model favored in England. The Spaniard, King Martin I of Aragon, King of Sicily in 1409, refused this latest proposal and Sicily remained under the tight control of the Spanish army at a time when other countries in Europe were developing an internal unity. Sicily instead was losing its political personality and its potential for becoming an independent state.

Under the rule of Spanish viceroys Sicily fell into obscurity for the next 300 years. The commercial and social integrity of the island continued to precipitate dangerously. Commerce and industry suffered. The silk industry was destroyed, agriculture and cattle-raising devastated. The countryside was threatened and controlled by bandits who had a dual function: some robbed the rich to help the poor, or pretended to help the poor and helped themselves; others served as henchmen for *latifondisti* who sheltered and protected them in exchange for subjugation of peasants; others probably functioned in both capacities. The coastline was open to piracy. Battles against the Turks, whose assaults against the Sicilian coastal areas had become far more frequent after their conquest of Constantinople in 1453, resulted in many acts of heroism by the Sicilians. However, the Sicilian navy, which had sailed the Mediterranean with a proud fleet in the days of Federico II, was so reduced in size that it was difficult to defend its borders successfully. Sicilians attempted to expel their oppressors with insurrections in Palermo and Messina but were overpowered by the large Spanish army garrisoned on the island.

Only under Alfonso V (1416-1458), who visited Sicily frequently, were some social, economic, and cultural improvements realized. To his credit was the founding of the University of Catania. He earned the loyalty of Sicilians during his forty-year reign. According to the historian, Christopher Duggan, the few social improvements were notable only when compared to the social and cultural desert of the previous two hundred years of French and Spanish rule. Unfortunately for Sicily, King Alfonso needed large sums of money to finance his wars against Naples. Ways and means were devised to raise funds. Creation of tributes and positions in high office, or indulgences for sale, were inducemenss for *latifondisti* to contribute large sums of money. Abundant new taxes were levied. Sicily ended by being forced to contribute more generously than any other part of the Empire to Alfonso's war campaigns.[62]

Ferdinand, the Catholic, succeeded to the throne of Spain in 1479, married Isabella of Castille, unified Spain and expelled the Moors. While his boats under the command of Christopher Columbus sailed towards the new world, Sicily was financing Spain's wars in Granada and against the Turks. In addition to carrying much of the financial burden for Spain's wars and explorations, Sicily was burdened with a succession of viceroys appointed by King Ferdinand who inflicted grave social, religious, and economic consequences upon the already troubled existence of the island.

In 1487, the Holy Office of the Inquisition was introduced in Sicily. Heretics were persecuted and punished during public *autos- da-fé,* or acts of faith, and the Inquisition pandered the *latifondisti* with positions of importance within the Holy Office in return for their loyalty. The edict of expulsion of Jews from Spain and Sicily was promulgated in 1492 against strong Sicilian opposition. Serious damage to the island's economy resulted as it was deprived of valuable Jewish artisan and middle- class citizens. During the unpropitious rule of the viceroy, Ugo Moncada, (1509-1516), the Holy Office became so powerful that the Inquisitors settled into the royal palace. Moncada incited rivalry and anger among cities, particularly Palermo and Messina, by granting Messina the right to coin money, which had been Palermo's privilege since 1432. To make matters worse, Messina demanded to become capital of the island in place of Palermo.

With the ascension of Charles V to the Spanish throne in 1516, Sicilians invited the hated viceroy to step down, but not only did he refuse, he declared the Sicilian Parliament dissolved.[63]

The popular uprising known as the "Second Sicilian Vespers" erupted in Palermo protesting this turn of events and the perpetual garrisoning of hated Spanish troops on the island. The viceroy was forced to flee to Messina and the Holy Office was driven out of the royal palace.

Despite these frequent acts of heroism, with no middle class, with forced failure of cities, and a powerful landed aristocracy, political fragmentation worsened. The stronger Spain became, the further Sicily was pulled away from the mainland of Italy and the splendors of the *Rinascimento*, and the further it was thrust into feudal obscurity.

Charles V of Spain was Holy Roman Emperor from 1519-1556. He was heir to Europe's leading dynasties – Aragon, Kingdom of Castille, Duchy of Burgundy, Hapsburgs of Austria. He also ruled over territories in western and southern Europe and colonies in the Americas. He divided his realms between his son, Philip and his brother, Ferdinand. His paternal grandparents were Emperor Maximilian I and Mary of Burgundy and his maternal grandparents were Ferdinand of Aragon and Isabelle of Castille whose daughter was Catherine of Aragon, the first wife of Henry VIII. After the death of his paternal grandfather, Maximilian, in 1519, Charles inherited the Hasburg lands of Austria. He was crowned Holy Roman Emperor in 1530 by Pope Clement VII. He was the last emperor to receive a papal coronation. As Holy Roman Emperor, Charles also ruled over the German states but his real power was limited by the princes, there. Protestantism was gaining strong support in Germany and Charles was determined not to allow this to happen in the Netherlands. An Inquisition was established in 1552 and all heretics faced the death penalty. He outlawed Martin Luther.

While Sicily had no interest in Spain's many wars against the French, Turks, Germans, and Dutch, the island was forced to contribute enormous quantities of gold, silver and grain. A good 1/3 of Sicily's total national income was assigned to Spain's defense, and 1/5 for "service to the King."[64] In its more glorious past Sicily had enjoyed a prosperous relationship with the Turks and North Africa. Ironically, during the reign of King Charles V, the island was made a Spanish base for attack against the African coast. The island was subjected to frequent attacks by the Ottomans aided by Sicily's hated enemy, the French, who were fighting alongside the Turks against their centuries-old enemy, Spain! (The Ottoman Empire, at the height of its power in the 16-17th centuries, spanned three continents, controlled much of southeastern Europe, the Middle East, and North Africa.)

Although her economy was floundering, Sicily reacted heroically to the call for European unity against the growing Turkish menace. The battle of Lepanto (Nafpaktos), in1571, one of the most heroic in the island's history, weakened Islam Turkey's offensives against Christian Europe. The Turks had conquered the island of Cyprus, the Venetian stronghold in the eastern Mediterranean and danger was imminent. Old rivalries and enmities were put aside by western Europe out of fear of a Turkish onslaught. Philip II of Spain allied himself to the Republic of Venice, the Papacy, the Savoy dynasty, and the Knights of Malta. Don Juan of Austria, a natural son of Emperor Charles V, and stepbrother of Philip II, was supreme commander of the combined forces.

By July 1, 1570, a powerful fleet of 207 ships sailed into Messina's harbor. Sicily's contribution was ten well-armed galleys which had been built by Sicilians with Sicilian funds. The Christian and Turkish fleets challenged each other at Lepanto, on the west coast of Greece, not far from Cephalonia. The naval battle lasted about ten hours and the Turks with their 300 ships were badly defeated. A good part of the victory is credited to the Sicilians. In fact, the Turkish encirclement of the Christian galleys was prevented thanks to the presence of mind and courage of the Sicilian Giovanni Cardona, captain of the vanguard ship *Capitana di Sicilia,* who, alone, faced 16 Turkish galleys, since the other lead ships, captained by the Genovese, Giannandrea Doria, had pushed too far ahead. It was left to the Sicilian ship and Captain Giovanni Cardona to upset the Turkish offensive and force the Turks to flee.[65]

By 1580 the decline of the Spanish Empire had begun and King Philip II was compelled to diminish the Spanish presence in the Mediterranean. As a result, Sicily was exposed more than ever to increasingly frequent attacks by pirates along its shores. Farms within ten miles of the shore were destroyed by piracy. Extensive damage to the island's foreign as well as domestic commerce resulted. Sicily became more and more vulnerable as these acts increased. Having had no autonomy in military affairs and no militia of its own, the island was poorly prepared to defend itself.

By the XVIIth century, disastrous deforestation, a result of the destruction caused by warring foreign armies, had started to take its toll. Soil erosion gradually upset and changed the direction of rivers and created floods. Fertile valleys were ruined by the spread of swamps and malaria.

This, together with continuing attacks of piracy and banditry, forced the farmer to seek higher and higher ground where steep, rugged slopes created an evermore violent cycle of soil erosion. Famines resulted.

After the death of Philip II in 1598 his son, the very inept Philip III, succeeded him. His reign (1598-1621) witnessed the start of a period of extreme catastrophe for the island. Corrupt and fraudulent practices in public administration, the severity of the Holy Office of the Inquisition, which manifested itself not only as an arm of spiritual repression but more and more as an arm of political repression, the numerous catastrophies (repeated famines and epidemics, including the bubonic plague which decimated the populations of Messina and Palermo) brought everything to a stop.

The Thirty Years' War, which began in 1618, was a war fought to alter the European balance of power. Sicily was forced to supply the Hapsburg-Spanish cause in Hungary and Germany large sums of money, which imposed other enormous financial burdens on an already ravaged island. Soldiers and galleys financed by Sicily were sent to fight against Spain's enemies, and great quantities of food were supplied to refurnish the Hapsburg troops in Lombardy and Alsace.[66]

Protests against administrative abuses and public attempts to install a different political regime ended in defeat. In 1641, the English ambassador secretly informed Spain that a plan for independence was being organized. By 1647, the situation was grave. The populace was faced with starvation. The result was an insurrection. No aid came from any foreign governments and the uprising presented no real danger to Spain. The internal divisions within Sicily, both geographic and social, prevented the development of strength and unity. The eruption of Etna, in 1669, destroyed eleven cities southeast of Etna and submerged part of Catania. A devastating earthquake in 1693 destroyed a good part of southeastern Sicily with a death toll of 59,700; in Catania alone, out of a population of 27,000, 18,000 perished.

As the century ended, so ended the reign of Charles II, who had ruled since 1665, came to an end. This concluded the direct line of Hapsburgs in Spain and Sicily, since no heir had been produced by Charles II. Following his testament, Spain and Sicily were transferred, along with much of his personal property, not to Hapsburgs, but to Philip of Anjou, a grandson of Louis XIV of France. So it came to pass that Sicily, for many years trapped by the Spanish Hapsburgs in a war against the French Bourbons, now found itself on the other side, once again a pawn of France. Philip's succession as King Philip provoked the wars of Spanish succession and intrigues continued in Europe. England, Germany, and Holland feared that Sicily would become an outpost of the French in the Mediterranean, and they plotted to make the Archduke Charles, an Austrian Hapsburg, King of Sicily.

In 1707 Austrian troops landed in Sicily when Spanish strength on the island was at its weakest. Simultaneously, Sicilians, hoping to take advantage of the moment to gain their independence, united in an uprising but were no match for a stronger adversary, and the insurrection quickly ended. Spanish troops regained control and many Sicilian rebels were tortured and killed. Austrians attacked along the coast, and the English Navy bombed Messina. In 1711 the Spanish viceroy in Sicily had to execute several of his restless officers, and, to set an example, he had their heads soaked in brine and then exhibited to the public.[67]

The Treaty of Utrecht / Sicily The Pawn

The Peace of Utrecht of 1713, a series of international treaties ending the war of Spanish succession in Europe, saw to it that a balance of power prevented the domination of the former Spanish- Hapsburg Empire by either Bourbon France or Hapsburg Austria . Philip V, the Bourbon grandson of Louis XIV of France, became king of Spain and its overseas colonies, as he renounced any claim to the throne of France. England acquired a thirty-year monopoly of the Spanish-American slave trade, Gibraltar, Minorca, Hudson Bay, Newfoundland and Nova Scotia. Austria received Milan, Naples, Sardinia and the Spanish Netherlands. Subsequently, through English intervention and to her advantage, since England feared a predominant French presence in the Mediterranean, Sicily was taken from Philip V of Spain and given to Philip's father-in-law, Vittorio Amedeo, Duke of Savoy, in Piedmont. Five years followed under the rule of Vittorio Amedeo, then fourteen years of Austrian rule, and, thereafter, Spanish-Bourbon rule from Naples.

When the Duke of Savoy arrived in Sicily in 1713 and, amidst solemn pomp and splendor, was crowned king in the Duomo of Palermo, he was greeted with optimism by the people. At last Sicily had a king who resided on the island. In February, 1714, the new king convened Parliament. Certain reforms were requested which he promised to examine. He attempted to understand local problems, but initiated only tentative, superficial reforms. Unfortunately, the crucial priorities, economic reform and social healing, so necessary after 300 years of Spanish misrule, were not addressed realistically. The new Piedmont government allocated the huge sum of 400,000 scudi for the king's appanage, while only 450,000 scudi was set apart to address all gravely needed public works for an entire island which was still reeling from the destruction of war, famine, and earthquakes.

Resentment was added to disillusionment as the king, totally unconcerned with Sicilian sensitivity, reshaped the government by placing Piedmontese and Savoyards, strangers to the island, in the highest offices. The condescending and critical approach of the northerners became an effrontery to Sicilian pride. In addition, although aware of the injustices of the baronial courts created by the *latifondisti* and the economic disadvantages resulting from uncontrolled baronial rule, the new king did little to reduce feudal abuses. His advice to his court was to avoid stirring up the *latifondisti* against each other and to prevent them from uniting.

Further complications doomed the king's reign. The power struggle between the papacy and the king left many citizens deprived of their religious comforts. The papacy, always closely allied to the French, encouraged Sicilians to defy royal authority. Their refusal to yield to the papacy and the hated French resulted in denial of Catholic rites. Privileges and immunities, built into society at every level, were insurmountable and greatly obstructed reform. An intolerable immunity, created to appease Philip V of Spain at the Congress of Utrecht, allowed him to retain possession of all his lands in Sicily, after he had surrendered his sovereign rights there. This included any land confiscated by the Spanish crown from private individuals on the island before 1713. Philip V retained personal property rights over, possibly, as much as 1/10 of Sicily after he had surrendered his sovereignty to the king from Savoy. His lands remained under the administration of Spanish officials, and he claimed exemptions from taxation, from ordinary laws, and from military service for all Spaniards remaining in Sicily. The privileges also included the employment of a separate police force.[68]

Within five years, political demands and unrest forced the new king back to Piedmont, and Count Maffei was appointed viceroy. The king took with him several most talented Sicilians, among whom were the legal expert Nicola Pensabene, the erudite scholar Francesco d'Aguirre, who later reformed the curriculum at the University of Piedmont, and the architect Filippo Juvarra from Messina, who beautified Torino with splendid monuments including the Basilica di Superga and the Castle of Stupinigi. The archives of the king's brief reign and several of previous reigns also went with him.

Sicilians were left with bitter memories of the Savoy reign. Excessive taxation which further drained the island and impoverished the people, painful spiritual controversy with the papacy, lack of tact in Savoyard rapport with the population, and the restriction of liberties previously enjoyed, such as freedom of the press, all contributed to the conclusion that the Savoy period was one of the darkest in Sicilian history. Even today, the Sicilian peasants, when faced with a spectacle of misery and desolation exclaim:

Pari ca cci passò casa Savoia!
"Looks like Casa Savoia has been here!"[69]

Both inner unrest and foreign attack precipitated the new king's return to the mainland. Spain's attempt to reconquer Sicily, which had been lost in 1713, resulted in a surprise attack in 1718 by the Spanish armada, near Palermo. The Savoyard viceroy Maffei and his entourage were forced to flee, leaving a Spanish viceroy appointed by Philip V of Spain to take over once again! Simultaneously, a popular uprising against the Savoyards ignited and became another independent thrust by the Sicilians to rid the island of unjust rule. The Savoyard troops who had sought refuge in Messina and Milazzo were forced to flee the island. The Spaniards succeeded in conquering Taormina and Messina. Their success was short-lived, however, since the English, looking after their interests in the area, defeated them in naval battles at Pachino in 1718.

In the power struggle against Spain, it became expedient for Austria, England, France, and Holland to create the Quadruple Alliance of August 2, 1718. Tragically for Sicily, Austria decided to respond to Spain's aggression by sending troops, and for one long year battles raged on the island between the armies of the Alliance and the Spaniards! In 1719 the Austrians defeated them badly at the battle of Francavilla. The retreating Spanish army carried off grain and cattle, destroyed valuable mulberry and other fruit trees and set fire to the woods. Near Palermo everything was cut down and destroyed. Sicily had once again become the battlefield of Europe.

Austrians took over Messina and Trapani in 1719, and Spaniards barricaded themselves in Palermo where, despite the treaty of Hague of 1720, which assigned Sicily to the Hapsburg Emperor, Charles VI of Austria, and assigned Sardinia to Savoy, hostilities continued until May 2, 1720. Soon after that date the Spaniards left the island.

As the war came to an end with the defeat of the Spanish, Emperor Charles of Austria became king of Sicily. The Treaty of London was drawn up and, once again, no one was concerned with the needs of Sicily. A large Austrian army imposed firm government. The battle-ravaged island was "milked for money" to refill the treasury of the bellicose Austrians, who had trespassed, used the island as a battlefield, and subsequently deprived it of its sovereignty.[70] Concurrently, the activities of the Holy Office became more merciless towards the populace, and judges of the Inquisition pronounced numerous and grave sentences in the name of religion.

The gravity of the tragedy is ironically and succinctly distilled in the following popular Sicilian verses:

Lu Santu Patri ni livau la missa,
lu Re conza la furca a li parrini,
currunu li funtani a stizza a stizza,
li terri mancu spicanu luppini!
Domini Diu li casi ni subbissa,
li jurati ni sucunu li vini,

Sicilia e' fatta carni di sasizza,
cca c'e' la liggi di li saracini![71]

"The Holy Father denies us Mass,
The King prepares gallows for our priests,
Our fountains barely drip a drop,
The earth's force sprouts hardly a bean!
The Lord God sees that our houses are buried.
Lawmakers drain the blood out of our veins,
Sicily's become chopped meat for sausage,
And we are ruled by Saracen law!"

The Spanish Bourbons / The Downward Spiral

Spain never relinquished its dream of re-conquering Sicily. When, in 1734, international tensions, precipitated by the Polish succession, led Philip V of Spain to ally himself to France and Piedmont, he invited his son, Charles of Bourbon, to Italy. In May of 1734 Charles conquered Naples and, on May 15, 1734, he was proclaimed Charles III, king of Naples and Sicily. He set out to conquer the island. The campaign was not long and the Austrians, now isolated from allies, retreated from the island. On June 30, 1735 Charles III swore to observe the laws of the kingdom and he initiated a series of reforms. Against their will, the Sicilians were united to Naples and made the pawn of a Bourbon prince of Spain. The populace hoped that the king would live on the island since he had sworn to preserve its laws, but he remained a short time only, and then returned to Naples to rule his kingdom from there. In Naples, Charles III created sumptuous palaces, public buildings, theaters, including the San Carlo Opera House. His aim was architectural development of Naples thus offering work to the unemployed and ending hunger.

Despite his return to Naples, the island enjoyed a fifty-year respite from decades of war and chaos under the peaceful reign of Charles III. He inherited an island devastated by two recent conquests, destroyed by war, reduced to extreme poverty, and in dire need of being rebuilt. Most importantly, besides economic viability, the people needed a rallying force, an ideal. Charles III was effective in restoring power to the Sicilian Parliament, in restoring some income earned from the island to the island, and in enacting trade and navigation agreements with Turkey and Tunisia. In 1752, unfortunately, he confirmed the abrogation of long-term farm leases without compensation to tenant farmers for capital improvements achieved by their ingenuity and hard work. This led to far-reaching disastrous consequences. (When in the 17th century some attempt was made at land reform, long-term lease holding was established by several latifondisti, and farmers acquired a bit of property of their own. Landless farmers were attracted to these estates since, for the first time, benefits were notable. Tenant farmers received the value of long-term improvements they themselves had produced, thus reducing the need to push the maximization of immediate return through disastrous over-cropping of the land. Latifondisti obtained rents from their leaseholders. Some improvement of the human condition was coming to fruition.)

The departure of Charles III from Naples in 1759 and his return to Spain for reasons of succession to the Spanish throne left his reign to his nine-year-old son, Ferdinand, under the tutelage of a council. The island was again governed by a viceroy as it tried to avoid the worst, already worn out by famines (particularly grave in 1763), pestilence, and sacking by bandits. Rioters in Palermo, excited into action by cries of "Bread! Bread! We want bread!," were eventually summarily executed without benefit of trial. [72] Unfortunately, under Spanish command, revolutionary ideals were crushed and social and constitutional reforms were quickly forgotten. The centuries-old problem of feudalism in Sicily continued to enslave the farmer.

One century later, the Spaniards found it expedient to allow *latifondisti* wide powers: many Spanish aristocrats in government were so indebted to them that their whole economy was in danger. Consequently, in 1752, during the reign of Charles III, when long-term leases were cancelled with no compensation to tenants for capital improvements, one vital incentive for agricultural development was lost. The resulting creation of squalid land-tenure contracts further plunged the landless farmer into despair, further enriched the *latifondisti,* and further increased their control over labor. Growth of smaller farms ended and day laborers and sharecroppers were hired to farm the large estates. The exploitive farming contract, the *gabella,* common in the past, was now reinstated. An overseer, the *gabellotto*, supervised the large estates and collected all taxes for the *latifondista* in advance.

Frequently foreigners, these *gabellotti*, became rich men. More ruthless than their landlords, they contributed to the further enslavement of the peasant who labored on a day-to-day, or at best, a short contract. By 1770 these tax collectors were referred to as the "new tyrants" of the Sicilian countryside. Taxation in advance forced the peasant to slaughter animals, cut down timber, plow up virgin territory, and over plant. A large class of industrious people was made useless to the state and to themselves.

Rents, taken by the absentee landlords, were not reinvested into the commonwealth of the island. One could travel for miles without seeing a farm house, a road, or a tree, because most of the profit from agriculture was spent by the *latifondisti* at their estates in Palermo. The topography of the island made the construction of a viable network of roads very costly. Economic survival depended upon this network but it was not accomplished. Viceroys and royal officials often overlooked misgovernment by landed aristocrats. They, with their *gabellotti,* had private armies of roughnecks whose job it was to compel obedience from recalcitrant peasants. The government recognized and even employed these private armies. [73]

Spanish Bourbons, ruling from Naples, began the elimination of feudalism in Naples during the 18th century, but, they knew that keeping Sicily submissive with the assistance of *latifondisti* would be less expensive and troublesome. With their forceful assistance of landowners, any act of rebelliousness or movement for Sicilian independence could be checked. They also could assist in the inculcation of respect for Church and State. The Bourbon government, in return for the political subservience of the *latifondisti*, was ready to excuse their malpractices. During this period of tremendous duress, unrest governed the populace. Uprisings were frequent.

During the reign of Charles III, from 1781 to 1794 Sicily was consecutively governed by two enlightened viceroys who, despite their failure to utilize emerging middle- class intellectuals, introduced several reforms. Palermo was beautified, a suburban cemetery was built outside the city, the forerunner of other such cemeteries throughout Italy, public security was strengthened, and certain useless costly celebrations among the courtiers were abolished. A most important reform was the suppression of the Holy Office in 1782 and the direction of its copious revenue to the creation of cultural institutes such as the astronomic observatory, the botanical gardens in Palermo, and the faculties of advanced mathematics and experimental physics at the university.

Tragically, these changes fell far short of the civil, economic, fiscal, and legislative reforms essential to save the island from desolation. The result was the continued deprivation of what should have been a positive, constructive, and proud society, plunging it further into futility and despair. The consequences were polarization and anarchy. Manipulation by a relentless presence of foreign rulers resulted in contempt for government and law by much of the populace. The difficulty facing any successive government was the problem of a polarized citizenry deprived of ideals, and deprived of faith in government. "The public good" had lost all meaning. By the early 19th century, lawlessness and despair saw the emergence of bands of outlaws who terrorized the island along with the henchmen of the *latifondisti*.

Money allotted for public works by Spanish Bourbons and parliament remained unrealistically inadequate while the pomp and circumstance, the extravagances, the palaces of reigning aristocrats continued to drain most of the wealth and produce nothing for the land. Roads continued to be in total disrepair or non-existent; mountainous terrain was inaccessible, and most remote areas remained isolated. Too many loopholes had been built into Sicilian commerce making any efficiency impossible.

Relentless arrival of foreign rulers had left behind a tangle of contradictory, un-codified legislation which was extremely difficult to decipher or apply. The deviousness, complexities, and delays led to civil contempt and the flouting of public justice. Individuals were forced to seek redress by other means. The poor could not afford the excessive costs and delays of lawsuits. Much of the population was persuaded to seek protection or assistance from those who demonstrated more practical efficiency than legal channels offered.

In their futile attempt to conceal the truth of the breakdown of law and order, the Spanish courts imposed harsh deterrent penalties on their subjects, which included branding, public torture, strangling, disemboweling of prisoners, and a permanent display of severed heads. The royal historian of the Spanish Bourbons, when describing the protests, the violence, and the legendary robber heroes of this time, remarked that they showed "characteristics which we deem rightly all part of the national character, and which remained the same whether under Spain, Savoy or Austria."[74] This repugnant perversion of the history of an oppressed people is being scrupulously reevaluated!

The Dream Awakening

In the early 19th century, while the Spanish reign was bringing further ruin to the island, many Sicilians were awakening to the idea of liberty. Revolutionary ideals found enthusiastic acceptance among Sicilian intellectuals. In 1795 a group of Sicilian patriots, professionals and educators, led by a noted judge, Francesco DiBlasi, planned an uprising with freedom and the creation of a Sicilian republic its goal. A spy revealed the plot to the Spanish viceroy which resulted in death for the revolutionaries. DiBlasi, after being brutally tortured for names of collaborators which he refused to reveal, was decapitated in Palermo in a public square while three of his companions were hanged. Many intellectuals, such as Francesco Crispi, lawyer and statesman, who were captivated by the emerging ideals of liberty and patriotism, came to realize that Sicily needed outside help to free itself from Spanish Bourbon rule. The relentless presence of foreign armies had left this small island with few professional soldiers, and therefore unable to liberate itself from foreign control without outside help.

In 1796 Napoleon led his troops successfully through northern Italy and on June 5th Bourbon troops were defeated at Brescia and armistice was imposed, leaving Austrians to battle the French alone. In two years, Napoleon's successes led to the formation of the Republics of Liguria, Cisalpina, and Rome. In 1798, with Napoleon away in Egypt commanding his troops there, despite the armistice of Brescia the Bourbon Kingdom of Naples, supported by the English fleet commanded by Admiral Horatio Nelson, was again at war with the French. Bourbon troops entered Rome to restore the papacy. As the French retreated, Ferdinand IV entered Rome with the pomp of a conqueror, but was soon forced to flee from a forceful French counter offensive and return to Naples. As Napoleon's army continued its march south and prepared to invade Naples,

King Ferdinand of the Two Sicilies, in Oct. 1798, boarded the Vanguard, Nelson's flagship, escorted by the Bourbon Royal Navy's Admiral Francesco Caracciolo's vessel , fled the French enemy and sailed to Sicily. The king took with him his entire family, along with much money from Neapolitan banks, and the royal treasure. Prince Pignatelli was assigned to represent the king during his absence.

Sicilians were moved by the arrival of their king and welcomed him warmly. Ferdinand and his queen lived settled into their palatial environment idling life away luxuriously in Palermo accompanied by Lady Emma

Hamilton and Lord Horatio Nelson. Ferdinand's queen, the Austrian Maria Carolina, who hated Neapolitans and Sicilians, had an insatiable desire for their money. While in Sicily she attempted to lay her hands on the road-building fund and she took deposits from charities and the Palermo bank. Ferdinand and his queen lavished estates and gifts on Sir William and Lady Hamilton, and Admiral Nelson received a feudal estate, Bronte, at the foot of Mt. Etna, which brought an annual income of 6,000 gold ounces.

Insensitive to the massacres of Jacobins (revolutionaries) and the suffering inflicted on his people in Naples, the king, queen and the lovers paraded themselves in Palermo in sumptuous costumes attending theater and masked balls.[75]

In February 1798, the first issue of "The Monitor" the official journal of the *New Republic* edited by Eleonora Fonseca Pimental, an intellectual noblewoman, once close to the royal family, appeared on the streets of Naples. Unfortunately, almost universal illiteracy among laborers and peasants prevented any fruitful circulation.

In 1799, Admiral Caracciolo returned to Naples to find a city where not only intellectuals, but also many aristocrats seemed infatuated by the new revolutionary ideals brought by the French. Among many, disillusionment and disappointment overcame their former support or respect for the monarchy; Admiral Caracciolo, too, became supportive of the idea of a republic. The Republic of Naples was proclaimed in January, 1799 after a popular uprising.

Tragically, for the Republic, the French were forced to leave the provinces and the city of Naples to confront defeats in the North to Austrian and Russian troops. Republicans struggled to defend Naples alone but defeat was unavoidable. Grass roots devotion to republican ideals could not be counted on.. Peasants and lower classes were hostile to intellectual ideals. The significance of the movement was lost to them. The Church was too powerful and too reactionary. Naples' powerful Cardinal Ruffo who had fled from the republic to Calabria where he took control as he did in Basilicata and Pugilie, gathered an army of disreputable followers called 'lazzaroni' and returned to Naples. He tightened the noose around the city by adding the Neapolitan rabble to his 'lazzaroni' to fight the "godless enemies of religion and family". (Lazzaroni were members of the lower class, street people herded together by a leader. They frequently acted collectively as a mob following the lead of a demagogue and had formidable influence in periods of social unrest and revolution.) During this period of revolutionary debacle, the Neapolitan rabble (unlike the "sans culottes" in Paris) were strongly monarchists and mob violence was directed at republicans and

Jacobin sympathizers. The Republic was doomed without a vital popular base supporting it and only the French army to protect it.

Cardinal Ruffo tightened his control with his infamous band of lazzaroni around Naples. Admiral Caracciolo, now defending the Republic as commander of the navy, fired upon the approaching English fleet of Admiral Nelson aiming to topple the new Republic and restore the monarchy.

The counter revolution initiated by the papal army and the English fleet under Nelson, plus unbridled violence by the masses, resulted in the eventual return of the Bourbon monarchy.

As the end neared, Caracciolo's attempt at flight failed; he was arrested, taken aboard Nelson's ship, tried and condemned to life in prison. The life sentence was changed to death by hanging, imposed upon by Admiral Nelson. (a vile insult to the nobility who considered hanging a humiliating death fit only for criminals and the rabble. The guillotine was for nobility.) Hanged from the mast of Nelson's ship, his body was unceremoniously cast overboard un-shrouded. The following day his cadaver was spotted floating in the sea by islanders from Santa Lucia and was buried there. The execution of Caracciolo remains a blot on the character of Horatio Nelson, Maria Carolina, and King Ferdinand IV.

In July, 1799, the Republic fell. Ferdinand IV reentered Naples in 1802.

Disillusionment among Sicilians spread vastly when they understood that their king was not concerned with restoring the Kingdom of Sicily, and that he was not a man of his word, but that he had come only to take temporary refuge. In 1802, thinking that the war was over, Ferdinand returned to Naples. However, he failed to abide by the peace pact signed with the French. Napoleon had by then overcome the defeat of his fleet at Trafalgar, and was already emperor of France and king of Italy. He decided to occupy the Kingdom of Naples again and install his brother, Joseph, as king.

Ferdinand fled to Palermo a second time in 1806, again seeking refuge from the onslaught of Napoleon's troops. Having revealed himself a sovereign who cared nothing for Sicily and a man who did not keep his word, Ferdinand was received far less enthusiastically the second time.

During the four years of the king's absence, the island had suffered another grain shortage and the resurgence of piracy. Ships from Tunis ravaged the coast around Sciacca and Agrigento. The Jesuits, expelled in 1767, returned to the island in 1806 and settled in again. With the king back in Sicily, Parliament reconvened and granted him the usual tributes which included 100,000 ducats for the queen, Maria Carolina. (This queen and her controversial sister, Marie Antoinette, queen of France, along with 14 siblings were born in Austria, the offspring of Maria Teresa and Francis Stephen,

Empress and Emperor of the Holy Roman Empire. The young life of Marie Antoinette ended in alleged elaborated accusations and final tragedy. Maria Carolina, who was known for perverted excesses and extreme cruelty, returned to Austria after the death of her husband, Ferdinand IV, where she was unceremoniously tolerated until her death, albeit, a natural death.)

Sicily again sustained much of the weight of the war against Napoleon, this time aided by the English who had formed a sort of protectorate over the island after several attempts by the French to land their troops. The coastal inhabitants, responding with spirit and courage and fighting alone, thwarted French attempts and pushed them into the sea.[76]

Pressure from *latifondisti* and the English, who influenced island policy strongly, induced Ferdinand IV to create a new constitution affirming the separation of Sicily from Naples. For a short period the Kingdom of Sicily came into being again. (Britain's need to keep the Mediterranean water routes free from the threat of Napoleon's Navy made Sicily an important strategic link and encouraged British support of the Kingdom of Sicily.) In 1811 Lord William Bentinck landed in Palermo to serve as England's plenipotentiary ambassador and for three years he shaped Sicilian politics. In 1812 the new Constitution prepared by the Sicilian jurist and scholar, Paolo Balsamo, was approved by Parliament and sanctioned by the King. Basing it on the English model, Balsamo's constitution established two distinct houses: the House of Lords and the House of Commons. Feudal privilege would be abolished and freedom of the press granted. The king would be prohibited from garrisoning foreign troops in Sicily without consent of Parliament, and he would be obliged to reside in Sicily or cede the throne to his son. Thus, Ferdinand IV of Naples and Sicily became Ferdinand III of Sicily.

By 1816, after the battle of Waterloo and the fall of Napoleon, Sicily's anti-Napoleonic function ended, and England withdrew her support. After Sicily had twice saved the Bourbon throne and had played an important strategic role in the anti-Napoleonic defense of the Mediterranean, the island was not represented and not defended at the Congress of Vienna which restored the throne of Naples to Ferdinand. He repudiated the newly approved Sicilian Constitution. Since he could not be a constitutional monarch in Sicily and an absolute monarch in Naples, he united the two realms again, and took the title of Ferdinand I, King of the Two Sicilies. This meant control from Naples again, once again making Sicily a province. Civilian councils were abolished, and all offices of importance were filled by King's decree as in the past. Any constitutional reforms again reflected the exploitive privileges restored to the Spanish Bourbon rulers. Since the welfare of the people was not an issue, all political, social, and economic reforms were ignored. Consequently, Sicilians lost their prerogative to be governed by their own regional administrators. Military conscription was imposed on them causing profound agitation among a people who had been traditionally exempt from military obligations and was constitutionally antimilitaristic.

Sicily felt particularly betrayed since the Constitution of 1812 had in part preserved her ancient privileges, respected the exigencies of her island mentality, and satisfied in part her continuous yearning for autonomy and independence. The rapidity with which this Bourbon duplicity occurred caused a spiritual break with Naples and eventually caused the Bourbons their throne. With their ironic poetic wit the Sicilians prophesied the Bourbon downfall by commenting on Ferdinand being IV, III, and I:

Fosti Quarto e insieme Terzo	"You were Fourth and Third together
Ferdinando or sei primiero:	Now you're Ferdinand number one
E se seguiti lo scherzo	If you continue with this game
Finirai per esser zero!	You'll end up being at last no one!"

Peasant unrest and opposition to Bourbon rule from Naples became the chief revolutionary forces on the island. Rebellions abounded: in 1820 and 1821 in Palermo, and in 1837 in Catania. They had at their core the separation from Naples and independence, but new insights and a vision of a united "Italy" were emerging. During the decade after the failed rebellion of 1820 many heroic Sicilian patriots were put to death in Bourbon prisons. As early as 1823 the first organized strike in Sicily occurred: bread bakers absented themselves from the work place and refused to return until a pay raise was granted.

Francesco I succeeded his father Ferdinand I in 1825. With his death in 1830, the throne went to his son, Ferdinand II, born in Palermo in 1810. In 1836, a cholera epidemic hit Naples and Sicily, interrupting all undertakings. In Palermo, deaths mounted to close to 2000 per day in a population of less than 200,000. The Bourbon government of Ferdinand II sent not one word of comfort, nor one bit of aid. There was chaos on the island. The epidemic claimed 70,000 victims; the worst was in Palermo, with 40,000 deaths, including 80 dead in public uprisings and 90 dead by firing squads. Hatred for the government and the King in Naples mounted.[77]

Despite the oppressive reign of Ferdinand II and nature's calamities, Sicily was improving its condition. Some construction of paved roads between communities was accomplished by citizens. Agriculture and commerce were reactivated with the export of grain, sumac, pistachio, wines, and sulfur. Some land reform in the shape of small landholdings was accomplished. Important contributions were made to science, philosophy, mathematics, economic science, politics, music, history, and literature. As early as 1827 a new approach to the care of the mentally ill was introduced. Ancient, barbaric chain-restraints were replaced by humane approach to mental health — the first time in Europe that an attempt was made at achieving a "mental cure."[78]

Some few changes were made possible by those who were becoming aware that in education, law, economics, and politics the established order could be improved. The idea of progress and responsibility started to take form among the educated, and a new cult of ideas was created. The Sicilian youth was educating himself with the works of the great Italian authors. Nevertheless, despite this new wave of enlightenment, many talented Sicilians continued to be forced to live in exile because of the chaotic political, social, and economic conditions at home.

One talented Sicilian who did not leave the island was Vincenzo Florio, founder of the Florio dynasty, who by 1841 owned an ironworks which employed 800 workers to whom he paid higher wages than those paid to workers up North.. By 1860, at the time of Garibaldi's arrival on the island, Florio owned a fleet of 14 ships. He was not only the economic benefactor of Sicily but also its spiritual leader for his audacious initiatives. In 1846 he inaugurated the first steamship line from Palermo, opening Sicily to Europe, and particularly to America and England. As early as 1832, he introduced Marsala wine to the world, making it the symbol of Italian hospitality. Florio increased sulphur production and exported it on his ships, he increased cultivation of sumac, created cotton and ceramic industries, enriched his bank, and continued to pay his workers higher wages than anywhere else in Sicily or Italy. His son, Ignazio, continued in these entrepreneurial enterprises with great success until family tragedy and worldwide competition destroyed what had been built. A sulphur crisis caused by unsustainable American competition, loss of citrus markets in Europe caused by competition from California, total destruction of the sumac industry because of innovative chemical preparations, ended the industrial dynasty and philanthropic ventures which had opened Sicily to the world.

The failed revolution of 1848 had taught that municipal rivalries were counterproductive and that unity was necessary in the cause of liberty and independence. Contacts were made with exiles who had fled the island to northern Italy after failed attempts at independence. Many political studies and proposals emerged, prepared by Sicilians of culture who had been in contact with the outside world. Many in Sicily adhered to Mazzini's *Giovani*

Italia and its belief in the unification of Italy as a republic. Political enthusiasm continued to grow among the professional and artisan middle class. By 1846 formal protests were sent directly to the Bourbon king. Odes to liberty, patriotic publications, hymns to Italy, to the Italian federation, and to the independence of Sicily abounded. Demonstrations were prohibited by the police, but public petitions and political letters circulated surreptitiously, requesting creation of a national guard and highlighting the basic ideas of the 1848 revolution: independence from Naples and the formation of an Italian federation.

A new force was now emerging unexpectedly, which added tremendous impetus and a new dimension to the Sicilian cause. The peasant population, unaware of politics and traditionally submissive, was becoming a powerful revolutionary force in their desire for a better life, for work, for land to cultivate, and for all those common benefits their forebears had been denied.

By January of 1848 many revolutionary pamphlets were circulating. One flier read, "Sicilians, the time of useless supplications has passed. Ferdinand has destroyed everything. We, a people born free, reduced to misery and in chains, shall we delay fighting for our legitimate rights? To arms, Sicilians! Unity will topple the monarchy!"[79.]

January 12, 1848, the date selected for the onset of the revolution, was the birthday of King Ferdinand II. The military governor failed to take seriously enough this threat by Sicilian patriots.

He did order that most government troops remain on the alert inside forts, armories, and surrounding the royal palace, while several platoons were deployed in the main squares and patrols were scattered throughout the streets of the city. Early the following morning, the 12th, a few cannonades were fired from the fort commemorating the king's birthday, and roads filled with people, unarmed, curious, expectant, and anxious. A youth appeared, and the signal was heard as he fired his rifle in the air. This grass roots revolution led by intellectuals, nobles, and professionals had started. Patriots addressed crowds with fiery words. With the ringing of the bells from the monastery of La Gancia, the revolt rapidly gained followers. Shops were hurriedly closed, people ran to arm themselves with whatever was available, and the first skirmishes started as Bourbon patrols quickly took their positions.

On the 15th of January violent bombing of the city began.

On January 21st, under extreme pressure, the king agreed to restore Sicily's Constitution.

As fighting continued, a provisional revolutionary council composed of 26 members was quickly formed. Ruggero Settimo (later considered the greatest Sicilian statesman of the 19th century) was elected president.

On the 25th of January the Provisional Council launched a proclamation declaring that Palermo, "on the 12th undertook a glorious revolution and was soon joined by many other cities that sent their brave, young men, ready to die for the cause of liberty. Current revolutionary sentiments in Europe, the actions of other Italians in the North, our strength and our unity all present the opportunity dreamed of for years by all Italians to claim our rights, to shed the ignominious burden of enslavement. We are entirely convinced that all the cities of our island will follow the example of Palermo, a city that has shown that its strength is in the people and nothing can resist the unanimous and voluntary agreement of the multitudes. The most respected Sicilians in our cities will now occupy public posts, provide for personal and property security, and recommend moderation.......... As they set up provisional committees, they are immediately in contact with the provisional council through their delegates, in order to imprint on the Sicilian movement the most prestigious solemnity."

Public funds were not touched to finance the revolution. Some members of the nobility and many wealthy families, churches and even Jesuits contributed large sums for the cause.

Jubilation was short lived as currents were shaping which would derail Sicily's success.Enthusiasm resulting from victory, followed by the eloquent words of Sicily's Provisional Council to its citizens, inspired and propelled liberal Neapolitan patriots, desperate for a constitutional monarchy of their own, to push dangerously for their own Constitution.

With this precipitation of events, the king, in order to avoid another revolution Naples, promised his Neapolitan subjects a statute and delegated his secretary of state to present a plan for approval within ten days. On February 24th, 1848, the Bourbon Constitution a reactionary statute which left power firmly in the hands of the monarchy, was presented to the Neapolitans and was, also, arbitrarily imposed upon the Sicilians.

Sicily's Provisional Council unanimously rejected this unfortunate turn of events announcing that it was the universal desire of Sicilians to unite with the Kingdom of Naples as "an independent ring in the chain of the Italian Federation." Sicilians demanded the reinstitution of their constitution. They demanded that their king resided on the island, that viceroys no longer governed them, that no Bourbon troops be garrisoned on the island, that they be joined as two rings, united but independent.

Ferdinand II insisted on one constitution for his entire reign. Sicilians insisted on one solely for Sicily. The Bourbon king granted a liberal constitution on the condition that Sicily accepted Bourbon sovereignty. In their enthusiasm, the revolutionaries failed to see the weakness of their position. They demanded autonomy. The Sicilian Parliament was convened and radicals and conservatives joined in a coalition government. The king's offer was formally rejected and a reply from revolutionary leaders declared that it was the desire of all Sicilians to be united with Naples as two equal rings of a beautiful Italian federation.

Giuseppe Mazzini's warm praise for Sicilians refers to this particular heroic moment: "Sicilians, you are grand! You have, in a few days, done more for Italy, our common fatherland, than all of us in two years of agitation....You have in a solemn moment of inspiration, listened to your conscience,...and your victory has changed Italy's destiny...God bless your army, your women, your priests, and you all!" [80]

Ministries were created and, until August of 1848, Ruggero Settimo was prime minister. In April of 1848 the most important act of his ministry was the declaration of the end of the Bourbon dynasty in Sicily approved by the unanimous vote of Parliament. The first act of Parliament was to confer the regency of Sicily on Ruggero Settimo. A new constitution was approved which was the most liberal of its day since it placed parliament above the king.

Delays and obstacles followed. Ambassadors to the mainland received words of praise and encouragement, but no concrete support for the Sicilian cause arrived. International politics was precarious. Absolute monarchies were threatened by rebelling subjects demanding a voice in their government. Pope Pius IX and the Piedmont court did not wish to earn the enmity of Bourbons who still considered themselves rulers of Sicily. Internal affairs were grave: funding for the revolution was disorganized and precarious, security on the island was weak, public order was becoming almost non-existent and was fomented by propaganda spread by Bourbon emissaries; bands of criminals created havoc.

Bourbon counterattack was imminent. In May of 1848, King Ferdinand II, having quelled the Neapolitan revolt and seen Piedmont defeated by reactionary Austria, judged that the moment was ripe for the re conquest of Sicily. He sent troops to attack the island again. Palermo fortified itself. Trenches were dug in Mondello. On March 29, 1849, eleven Bourbon warships docked in the port of Palermo. Messina was destroyed by bombardment and fires. Atrocities against citizens by Bourbon soldiers caused public censure from foreign consuls. Admirals Parker and Baudin, threatening an English and French armed intervention, imposed an armistice until March 29, 1849, to allow the government of Sicily and the King of Naples to reach an accord. In the interim the island was left defenseless, poorly organized, with too rapid a succession of events, and too many conflicting pressures.

The 1848 revolution ended with undignified capitulation and unconditional surrender. What had been a courageous and patriotic citizen uprising was not well understood and remained unaided by spectator countries. It was dragged down by leaders who were unprepared and weakened by contradictory ideals as chaos overpowered them. Delay by the newly-formed coalition government to build an army was fatal. Lack of funds led to total collapse. It had been hoped that help would come from Italian states or England and France, but none came. Many ministers resigned as the capitulation of the fledgling government became reality. The revolution had been a very costly experience.

It was soon after these distressful times that Karl Marx wrote, in the *New York Tribune*, in May, 1860, "In all human history no country or no people have suffered such terrible slavery, conquest and foreign oppression, and no country and no people have struggled so strenuously for their freedom as Sicily and Sicilians."[81]

Sicily never forgave Ferdinand II, not even after his death in 1859, clearly noted here in the island's epitaph:

Qui giace Ferdinando, a cui natura
die' cor di sangue, mente bieca e dura;
vil soldato, empio re, principe avaro
dall'Italia aborrito, all'Austria caro.[82]

"Here lies Ferdinand, from Nature gifted with
A bloody heart, a mind depraved and cruel;
Cowardly soldier, wicked king, miserly prince,
Abhorred by   , adored by Austria."

The last Bourbon king to rule Sicily was Francis II who came to the throne in 1859. Of this new king it was quickly said in Sicily:

Cicciu nasciu — so matri muriu,
Cicciu si maritau — so patri cripau,
Ora ca è re — viditi chi c'è! [83]

"Ciccio was born — his mother died,
Ciccio was married — his father croaked.
Now that he's king — beware! What's next?!"

The Fight for Freedom: Unification

Years of political unrest followed the return of Bourbon rule in Sicily. What had been a courageous citizen uprising had, regrettably, remained unsupported by spectator countries and, remaining isolated, was doomed to failure. It was dragged down by leaders unprepared by, and weakened by, contradictory ideals, and an enemy whose military might on land and sea dwarfed the grass roots weapons accumulated furtively by Sicilians preparing for the first shot to be fired.

Insufficient time for the newly formed Sicilian Council to build an army was fatal. Lack of funds led to total collapse.

The aborted revolution had taught a costly lesson; aid from outside was the only hope for success in future attempts at independence.

A decade had passed since patriots had battled to free their island from arbitrary foreign yolk, but their desire to expel their oppressors had not died in the failed attempt. Their revolutionary ideals were encouraged by the news that General Giuseppe Garibaldi, the free-lance revolutionary, was preparing to unify the peninsula and Sicily into an Italian republic. The plan was to free Sicily and southern Italy from Bourbon rule and form a new nation.

Sicily was to serve as the launching pad for the unification which would lead to the creation of the Republic of Italy. These republican ideas were not corroborated by the Savoy King Victor Emanuel II of Piedmont or by his prime minister, Cavour, even though they agreed with Garibaldi's plan to oust the Spanish Bourbons from Sicily and Naples. They did not agree upon a republic of Italy. They had other plans, but, for the moment, Garibaldi was useful. However, doubts burdened the Savoy monarchy. How far would Garibaldi continue his military and political journey northward, and once accomplished, how much of the occupied territory would he be willing to deliver to them?

Giuseppe Mazzini, the republican patriot, whose political philosophy was the catalyst for the revolutionary movement, inspired Garibaldi to act when the moment was right. Mazzini's "Giovane Italia" was the training ground for the coming struggle for a free and united republic. Sicilian exiles, living in the North, were collaborating with their northern allies and communications and planning had intensified with Sicily over the past decade.

Citizens were again beginning to rally; Revolution was in the air, word of Garibaldi spread quickly. News of his imminent arrival unleashed a new burst of patriotic enthusiasm and determination. Wherever clandestine gatherings were held, talk of Garibaldi, the Italian hero, fired the enthusiasm of patriots and ignored the real threat of yet another foreign presence in Sicily, which would simply replace the Bourbon presence. But, that too, would be confronted later. Their enthusiasm for Garibaldi's expedition was fueled by his Italian heritage and their admiration for his past heroism.

By the end of 1859 some of the most active exiles had returned secretly to the island to propagandize Garibaldi's program. Among them was Francesco Crispi, perhaps the most fervent disciple of Mazzini's republican ideals, a lawyer whose ideas clashed with conservative aristocrats and with the philosophy of power adhered to by the extreme right. Crispi met with leaders of youth bands, fugitives from Bourbon military police. Youths who were social outcasts or political rebels who could no longer find employment and had exiled themselves from communities they had lived in, making the hills their home.

He reorganized revolutionary committees as he visited major cities, concluding with Palermo, where, in a reunion with leaders, the name day of the king, October 4th, was selected as the date for the onset of hostilities.

Once again, as in 1848, Sicilians had selected a Bourbon holiday to initiate their revolution.

Revolutionary leaflets were circulated, as in 1848, throughout the island. Initially, the military police succeeded in controlling skirmishes in and around Palermo, but Bourbon troops were not skilled in battle in the countryside where patriots were hard to find. In Messina, Bourbon troops faced another uprising, as they did in Ragusa, Trapani, Cefalu, and other cities where troops were also ambushed and fired upon. Telegraph lines were cut, causing panic as Bourbon authorities were left without information about the position of their troops. On the contrary, news of revolutionary activity was circulated quickly and secretly throughout the entire island. Evidently, communication also existed between insurgents within the city and peasants in surrounding areas. At last, peasant unrest had become a powerful force for revolt. The once passive, exploited peasants had found their voice in their struggle for food, land, and social justice. Their protests were heard as they, too, began demonstrating and demanding "bread, land, water for their fields."

Aristocrats and moderate conservatives, who had led the 1848 revolt, kept a low profile this time. Those among them who would have considered a revolt, hesitated as they awaited an assurance of aid from abroad. Some members of the aristocracy fled the city when the first battles were fought, fearing that the insurrection would fail....or perhaps some fearing that it would succeed and the island would become part of Garibaldi's republic.

By 1860, revolution was in the air. A grass roots movement was essential if the large Bourbon army in Sicily was to be defeated. Garibaldi understood that the time was right to set sail for Sicily, where the war which would unify Italy had started. Sailing with him from Quarto, near Genoa, were about 1,000 men, his "Mille." Nino Bixio was captain of the *Piemonte* and Salvatore Castiglia, from Palermo, was captain of the *Lombardo*; his machinist, also from Palermo, was Giuseppe Orlando, the future industrialist, founder of the shipyard in Livorno. When Garibaldi landed, in Marsala, 3,000 Sicilian volunteers quickly joined him. From the will of the Sicilian people he received the strength to go on to victory, defeating the Bourbons in a surprisingly short time.

After heroic victories against the enemy throughout the island, the historic battle of Palermo was fought. Joined by hundreds of volunteers led by Antonio LaMasa, from Palermo, who had regrouped in the hills above Palermo, Garibaldi led the attack to enter the city. After a furious battle at Ponte Ammiraglio on the River Oreto and again at Porta Termini the Garibaldini entered Piazza Fieravecchia. A citizen uprising aided the 'red shirts' against the entrenched enemy who were also bombarding the city. Little has been said of the courage and loyalty of Sicilians, men and women, in their support of Garibaldi and freedom. Citizens of Palermo fought alongside the "Mille", struggling to free their island from tyranny. Under bombardment from the enemy casualties mounted. Aid was desperately needed and citizens offered all that they had. Disregarding personal danger, physicians set up emergency medical stations. Women, both privileged and poor, nursed the wounded. Food, linens, and beds were supplied. Medical supplies were few, but all was made available. There were many acts of courage and humanity.[85]

After Bourbon defeat in Palermo, and again at Milazzo and Messina, troops were commanded to withdraw. This time the Bourbon king eagerly agreed to an armistice. Joyfully, and with dignity, Palermo witnessed the retreat of the enemy. It was a time of elation for the incredible victory.

Garibaldi, who had proclaimed himself dictator and ruled for five months on behalf of King Vittorio Emanuele of Piedmont had awakened many fears and doubts in the minds of many Sicilians, but his personal charm and his genuine appeal to the common people won him immediate support among those who desperately needed a hero. In a deliberate appeal to peasants, he quickly abolished the hated tax on milled wheat and promised eventual land grants to the poor and to those who took arms. His program of reforms, under the advice of Francesco Crispi, included the nationalization of church property, land redistribution, the damming of rivers, reforestation of mountainsides, cultivation of wastelands, construction of the first Sicilian railway, and construction of schools. Norms were implemented for the collection of taxes on public property. Vagabondage and begging were outlawed. The poor were put to work clearing the ruins of war and rebuilding. A committee was nominated to research the island's artistic patrimony. The blueprint for reform was excellent, but, too much polarization and Garibaldi's total involvement in continuing his war on the mainland to follow his dream of a united Italy, took him from the island, and caused the plan to fail.[86]

His departure left little time to implement Francesco Crispi's economic and social plans for Sicily. Further complication was the appointment of Agostino DePretis, by the Savoy King's Prime Minister, Cavour, in agreement with Garibaldi, to replace him during his absence from the island. To make matters worse, De Pretis was an adversary of Francesco Crispi's republican ideals and favored the annexation of Sicily to the kingdom of Piedmont. To the disillusioned, he became known as Garibaldi's pro-dictator.

Furthermore, opposition to Garibaldi's reforms for the island emerged. *Latisfondisti* fought his ideas for agrarian and social reforms. Many citizens were offended by his dictatorship which reminded them of the Bourbon reign from Naples.

Many volunteers found it unacceptable to continue their fight on the mainland with Garibaldi's troops for a cause which had become only partially meaningful to them. Another threat came from peasants, forever deprived of any rights to the land. Garibaldi's promise to redress these wrongs, followed by extensive delays as he left the island to fight on northward, led to tragic disillusionment and fury which motivated spontaneous, forceful, and often violent occupation of portions of the *latifondi* by peasants. Garibaldi's lieutenant, Nino Bixio, came down so hard on these civic uprisings that land barons began to side with and support Garibaldi. The brutal repression inflicted upon peasants and leaders of the uprising by Bixio, and his soldiers, prompted a comment in an English newspaper stating that "No savages in the most barbarous parts of Africa ever treated their prisoners with more summary violence than Piedmont troops have in Southern Italy."[87]

The liberation of southern Italy was rapid and in a short time Garibaldi entered Naples victoriously. With the Bourbon government ousted, Garibaldi returned to Palermo.

Satisfied that very little Bourbon resistance remained on the island, Garibaldi relieved DePretis of his duties and appointed Antonio Mordini to replace him as he set off for the mainland again. Mordini's task was to pacify the aristocrats and conservatives who feared the idea of a republic, and appease republicans led by Crispi who strived to delay annexation as long as possible.

A commission of nobles, fearing republican victory, left for Turin to expedite Cavour's offer of annexation. Unbeknownst to them Cavour had already planned his move. He planned to remove his political foe, Garibaldi, from power as soon as possible and sent the regular Piedmont army into the Marches region (on the mainland) to surround Garibaldi and his volunteers before the General attacked the Pontifical States which stretched from Rome across the peninsula to the Adriatic. The General was convinced that immediate annexation of the South was a necessity since danger of war with Austria and France existed if he were to attack the Pontifical States.[88]

Fearing that all would be lost if he proceeded with his plan for a republic, Garibaldi convinced Crispi that annexation of Sicily to the Kingdom of Piedmont was the better route.

Consequently, the Constitution of Sardegna was forced upon Sicily and the entire body of Sicilian law was abrogated. Added to the chaos of the revolution, the new government, and the incoming army from Piedmont, was the bewilderment, the confusion caused by government imposition of the lira as the island's new currency, and the metric system of weights and measures. Yet no provision was made for local government. Piedmont laws and institutions were enforced without consultation with citizens instead of reviving the island's centuries-old Sicilian Parliament. It was becoming obvious that there was to be no autonomy but simply an annexation of the island to Piedmont.

With Garibaldi defeated and removed from command by the more astute diplomatic tactics of Cavour, the annexation of Sicily was formulated in Naples, not Sicily. By 1860, in an otherwise very fragmented society, almost everyone on the island had come to favor some kind of regional self-government. Most were willing to accept a political tie with the rest of Italy, since it was thought that only northern Italian help could protect the island against a Bourbon counterrevolution. A plebiscite in Sicily resulted in a vast majority of the limited, enfranchised-vote in favor of a united Italy, which in effect had already happened. Total power was transferred to Piedmont and Cavour. Sicilians, for whom Garibaldi was still a hero, were offended and dismayed. The worst offense was Cavour's denial of regional self-government. There was to be no Sicilian autonomy at all. On December1st, 1860, King Vittorio Emanuele II of the House of Savoy of Piedmont, arrived in Sicily for a brief sojourn and then returned to his kingdom in northern Italy.

A committee of eminent Sicilians recommended the establishment of a regional assembly with considerable powers. The recommendation was favored by most politically aware Sicilians. Unfortunately, eighty-five years had to pass before the Italian government accepted this advice. Cavour continued to hold out the promise of self-government, but, in private, he instructed his public officials to ignore local opinion. Piedmont laws were introduced at once without discussion and, when necessary, with force.

The first few years of Italian unification failed create a bond between the Savoy government and Sicily. Instead of an administration which looked to rebuilding the ruins of war and healing

psychological scars, both essential for the achievement of a well-ordered society, a military government was imposed. Instead of tackling the gravity of all facets of the economy, commerce, agriculture, industry, a few token miles of railway tracks were built. No attempt was made to bring the benefits of a national government to the island. It seemed that the aim was to make Sicily and the rest of Italy forget that Sicilians had fought heroically and then by plebiscite had voted for national unity. It appeared that, on the contrary, an image of a people averse to accepting the new government was projected. As rebellions increased, the General sent to put down the rebels reported that insurgents had crucified soldiers, burnt police alive, and sold the flesh of carabinieri on the marketplace. The general, himself, later admitted that the allegations had been no more than gossip but the image of the islanders remained critically tarnished.

Brutal retaliation by government troops followed quickly. Villages were burned to the ground on suspicion that food and shelter were being supplied to rebels, and as little as an insult to the national flag or to the King was enough to justify death to the offender. The result was hatred and fury.[89]

A state of siege by Piedmont troops existed. Uprisings continued. By 1863 dissatisfaction had increased among the Garibaldian republicans who believed that their national cause had been betrayed. Armed bands roamed around the capital and confrontations with Savoy troops occurred frequently. Insurrection was feared and many patriots were arrested only because they disapproved of the direction of the government. *En masse* arrests of Garibaldi's followers were frequent and they were grouped together with common criminals. Patriots were persecuted with violence and any faith in the new regime was destroyed. Brigands took advantage of the chaos to further their own criminal activities. To ensure that the heroic part played by the Sicilians in the island's liberation from Bourbon rule and in the unification of Italy be erased, all manifestations involving Garibaldi and his followers — even theatrical — were prohibited. [91]

Seven years of military service was forced on a population traditionally exempt from conscription. Reaction was strong and many attempts were made to escape the imposition. It was a special hardship for peasants who needed their sons on the farms. The government, more than ever, was thus identified with centuries of despotic and exploitive rule. Distrust deepened and led to increased loyalty to family and village. A wall of silence grew. Increasingly, Sicilians refused to testify against compatriots to a government for which they felt no loyalty nor trust. Local problems were solved more and more frequently among the citizens themselves.

In 1867, excessive laws against brigandage caused insurrections throughout the entire island. Citizens protested that laws were offensive and that all that was needed to destroy brigandage were local laws and orderly police control. Lacking understanding of the island's complex problems, the new Italian government assumed that repression would solve everything. Martial law was declared, and full powers were given which allowed military tribunals to shoot people on the spot. Arrests were made without trial. Hostages were taken in order to coerce citizens into obedience. Torture was sometimes used, as was the threat to cut off water supplies in the summer heat. Civil war was raging but enforcement of martial law was blamed on "brigandage" which failed to conceal the truth that the island was desperately fighting for survival.[92]

The profound miseries suffered by Sicilians, the refusal of the new government to grant parliamentary representation to minority groups — adherents of Garibaldi, Mazzini's republicans, conservatives, those seeking autonomy — led to a new revolt in Palermo with the battle cry of "Long Live The Republic!" The result was many deaths by firing squad.

Fundamentally, it was a social revolt brought to a head by workers whose standard of living was so dangerously low that they were desperate enough to abandon all caution. Diverse political groups joined together with workers in a battle for economic and social reforms. For one week Palermo fell into anarchy. The Italian navy also arrived and bombed Palermo into submission. Thousands of troops arrived from the mainland and since the profound social causes for these revolts were never addressed, an army remained on the island to maintain discipline for the next ten years.

Sicily's economy was reduced to a deplorable state. The new government in the North did not address the problems of farmers who were unemployed six months of the year. Northerners had no interest in protecting southern industries which might prove competitive with their own. The Piedmont government implemented rigid tax increases and the detested tax on milled wheat was reapplied. An austerity program disadvantaged the South and accelerated its industrial and economic decline. The silk and textile industries were eliminated to favor northern industrialists who were opposed to the annexation of the South. Powerful American competition brought Sicily's sulfur industry to its knees and decimated its European citrus fruit markets. Far from being brought into modern industrialization, Sicily's standard of living worsened dangerously. Taxes took money away from southern agriculture for investment, "increasing deliberately a regional disparity which was already dangerous," according to Mr. Mack Smith.

It was soon clear that although Sicily's tax burden, together with that of other southern regions, was excessive and disproportionate when compared to central and northern regions, Sicily and the South were only minimally subsidized by the government while central and northern regions received far more generous allocations. The Italian state spent 93 lire annually for every citizen of Lazio, 71 lire for citizens of Liguria, and only 19 lire for each citizen of Sicily.[96]

The North's built-in advantages, proximity to export markets, better communications, more skilled labor, cheaper available power, plus fiscal wealth pouring in from the South, made Torino, Milano, and Genoa great centers of productivity. With these advantages and disadvantages in play, the huge economic gap between North and South increased for the next 75 years.

The Dream Tormented / Mafia Image Magnified

The *leitmotif* of Sicily's modern history has been an endless quest for liberty and autonomy. Unity with Casa Savoia and Italy was acceptable but only with regional home rule and separate parliaments. In their 1876 exhaustive study of Sicilian economic and social conditions, Sydney Sonnino and Leopold Franchetti concluded that "Sicily, free to self-govern, would find the remedy for its ills. . . . we are assured of their success by the intelligence and energy of her people and the immense wealth of her resources."[97]

By the end of the 19th century, a profound sense of distress had intensified among the workers. Socialism had spread rapidly among the working classes. Some peasants now knew how to read and write, and those who had gone into the military service away from the island had been in contact with an outside world which focused on new needs and new expectations. A large and educated class of professionals was also ready to express its frustrations and unify its efforts.

Revolutionaries favored the socialization of land and mines. The *Fasci*[98] movement which emerged in 1873 brought together workers and peasants in a Socialist-directed movement. For the first time in the island's history, workers were discovering that they could organize themselves against abuses, and that sometimes success could be achieved through strikes. As a result, centuries-old domination by *latifondisti* was now being threatened by peasant strikes and union strength. Between 1888 and 1894, membership in the *Fasci* expanded and exceeded 350,000 Sicilian farm and sulfur workers. During the winery crisis in 1892, caused by the cancellation of a trade agreement with France, a petition was presented to the police commissioner outlining Sicilian socialist ideology: apportionment of public and uncultivated lands, reduction of taxes, and, most important, regional autonomy. Soldiers started firing on the crowd killing many of those demonstrating for a reply to the petition, and the peaceful demonstration turned into open revolt. It was the responsibility of Francesco Crispi, then prime minister of Italy to send 40,000 soldiers under the command of General Morra. The *Fasci* were outlawed and mass arrests without trial followed. The Socialist revolts of 1893-1895 ended with centuries of prison sentences for many of its members. Perhaps intimidated by the government of the North and fearful that the *Fasci* movement was becoming anarchical, Prime Minister Crispi failed his fellow-Sicilians by refusing to support the socialist ideals to which he, himself, had adhered in the past. In 1893, instead of promoting reforms and legislation which addressed social problems at their roots, he forcefully put an end to worker protests on the island and elsewhere. The troops he sent imposed martial law and quelled any unrest. British historian, Christopher Duggan, states that "the landowners and government were terrified by the expression of peasant militancy and, as in 1866, they tried to criminalize it. The outbreak of social unrest in Sicily, in 1892, was greeted with demands for the suppression of *brigandage*, even though there seems to have been only one bandit gang to speak of at the time."

Social outcasts, outlaws, some of the unemployed, together with social reformers joined together;

Under cover societies became powerful. The Sicilian felt compelled to look for protection to friends who had the capability of improving his condition or, at least, to ward off disaster. This assistance was given either in return for a past service or for future subservience by "men of honor" who now came to be called "mafiosi" because they were powerful and commanded respect. By the 1870s it was clear that criminality on the island was associated with political corruption and that the North, instead of improving the situation, had worsened it. Foreign journalists had begun to attack northern Italy for its lack of interest in dealing with the problems of the South and even for its ignorance of those problems.

Despite some steps forward, the land still remained in the hands of the *latifondisti* and they, in general, continued to delay land reforms. Some concerned landbarons had clearly demonstrated that it was possible to bring notable improvements to the land and to society. Nevertheless, as late as 1910 several hundred of the *latifondisti,* who represented less than one tenth of one percent of the total population, still owned half of the island and had little intention of improving the land with much needed irrigation, drainage, and construction of farmhouses. About 50% of the population was still illiterate at the turn of the century, and the three universities on the island produced only lawyers and bureaucrats, while urgently needed practical studies such as agriculture and engineering were neglected.

The national tariff policy of Italy continued to work insidiously against the South. The reduction of protective duties after 1861 allowed foreign textiles into Italy, ruining Sicilian textile manufacturers who could no longer compete with foreign imports. After 1878, and again in 1887, protective tariffs were reintroduced for the sole purpose of aiding the already industrialized North since there were no southern industries left to benefit from them. Some Sicilian politicians approved of this tariff since the *latifondisti* simultaneously obtained a duty on imported grains, which was a hidden subsidy that encouraged cultivation of wheat at the expense of cattle breeding and cultivation of vineyards and orchards. It delayed the splitting of *latifondi* and encouraged the already excessive cultivation of grains on unsuitable lands. Sicily was hit with a hail of taxes, community tax, provincial tax, surtax, family tax, mill tax and, finally, the inheritance tax. With their usual ironic humor the Sicilians bantered that now they had become "relatives of the king," since at their death the Italian government would inherit part of their money![99]

The central government failed to provide essential public services. Sicily had 10% of the population of Italy and received less than 3% of government expenditures for desperately needed irrigation and water control. Thirty years had to pass before the main roads that traversed the center of the island were completed. As a consequence, half the towns had no access roads and some had difficult access even by horse. The almost total isolation which existed crippled or halted progress.

Mass emigration which would eventually take more than four million Sicilians away from their homes was about to begin. It was not hunger alone that drove citizenz away. It was the despair and outrage directed at a new government which had failed them so badly. It was the many futile attempts to achieve freedom and self-determination. It was the repressive measures used to stem political and social reform. The dismemberment of a people, whose love of family and land was proverbial, was about to begin.

The Meaning of Mafia

At this time in Sicily's history, the "Mafia" was much publicized, and its image was magnified in order to help justify the government's policies in the South. Crime was exaggerated and attributed to the Mafia. The historian, Christopher Duggan, points out that "from 1863 to 1871 growth of crime was less in Sicily than elsewhere in Italy, and, relative to its population in 1871, the island stood seventh in the table of national crime statistics." He goes on to say, "The image of Mafia was created to suit the needs of Piedmont."[100]

(The etymology of the word mafia *presents several possibilities. One lies in its similarity to the Tuscan word,* maffia, *meaning misery, the other with the French word* maffier, *meaning devil. The word also has been traced to Arab words meaning "cave" and "place of refuge." Sicilians who rebelled against authorities during the days of Arab rule took refuge in caves. According to Prof. Santo Correnti in his Breve Storia della Sicilia, the word, which in 1862 entered common use in Sicily, derives from the Tuscan word,* maffia, *meaning misery or showy ostentation, and was introduced into Sicily soon after Italy's unification. He believes that organized crime began*

in Sicily during the Spanish domination from 1500 on. He recounts the humorous legend of three Spanish brothers who for the love of justice transferred themselves from Spain to southern Italy and founded the camorra *in Campania, the* 'ndrangheta *in Calabria, and the* mafia *in Sicily. Prof. Correnti states that the Spaniards as early as the 15th century had their "society of honorable men" which they transferred to their Italian possessions, including Lombardy. This can be seen in Manzoni's I* Promessi Sposi *set in 1628 in a society that is mafioso on all three levels: rural boss, don Rodrigo; middle level, the Unnamed One; at the top, the Count, each with his consiglieri, bodyguards, and killers.*

Giuseppe Pitrè[101] affirmed the existence of the word in the 19th century in a section of Palermo called "il Borgo". There the word mafia *meant beauty, graciousness, perfection, excellence: a pretty girl appearing to be aware of her beauty, having an indefinable aura of superiority was* mafiusa; *a house which was nicely furnished, clean, orderly, and appealing was* na casa mafiusedda. *Cleverness and bravery soon were added to the connotation of beauty and superiority. When applied to the male, the connotation included a sense of security, excessive boldness, but never defiance or arrogance. The* mafiusu *taken in this context was not a threat to anyone.)*

In 1863, a Palermo playwright, Giuseppe Rizzotto, wrote *I Mafiusi di la Vicaria,* several scenes of life in a Palermo prison; the habits, customs, and speech of *camorristi.* [102] The play was a great success throughout Italy for many years. It was then that the word *mafia* and the behavior of these prisoners became popular and well known to all classes of Italians, including journalists, politicians, and members of the new government.[103]

Mafia, having entered the Italian language, became synonymous with brigandage and *camorra* without being either. Brigandage became involved with open opposition to social and political injustices. In Calabria, the brigands, known as 'Ndrangheta, whose operation — smuggling and robbing — was carried out in the rough country inland, were joined by many who opposed the new government's partiality to the North, and brigandage took on the role of guerilla warfare against political oppression. The *camorra* of Naples, on the other hand, were secret gangs engaging solely in extortion, blackmail, kidnapping, and murder. Their activity was not involved with social or political protest.[104]

At the end of the 19thcentury, in Sicily, the Piedmont government jailed political and social activists without trial and, linking them to common criminals, conveniently labeled them 'mafiosi'.

The Hemorrhage of Emigration

As disillusionment and outrage deepened, as hunger increased and living conditions became ever more intolerable, as political and social activists realized that government bombs were more powerful, a great hurting mass began readying itself to break away from its homeland. By the late nineteenth century more than a million Sicilians left the island, altering it and its people forever. They were forced to leave what they loved most and sail to distant destinations to seek a better life. The majority reached the shores of North and South America to find, very frequently, that often hostility and hardship greeted them.

By 1907, despite the suffering and loss caused by the departure of so many, Sicily was receiving the incredible sum of one hundred million lire arriving annually through private remittances, from emigrants to their families left behind. Never before in the tormented history of the island had money ever poured back into the island rather than away as the booty of foreign rulers.[105]

Far from escaping into oblivion in their new and often hostile environments, the Sicilians labored endlessly long hours, often suffering injustices and denigration, as they continued to hold onto their dream of family and a better life. The more fortunate were finally joined by their families and the drama of assimilation in a new land began. Many eventually returned to visit or stay.

By 1910 "Americani" began to return home and buy land with their savings. They also brought back a sense of achievement and experience which began to free them from despair and resignation. They were able to build a life for themselves. On the island the shortage of manpower created by the exodus favored workers. *Latifondisti* were finally forced to consider the needs of the peasants whom they now had to coax to work the land. Some lands were finally converted to pastures and woods and, most important, the *latifondisti* finally faced the fact that they could no longer allow an agriculture which favored unemployment and led to erosion and soil impoverishment. The absentee landowners came to understand that their presence was necessary on the land to control its administration and to replace the hated *gabellotti*. They were now willing to sell some of their land to the more capable farmers or to agree to more favorable leasing contracts.

In eastern areas of the island where less criminality existed, more opportunity for honest progress was available. In the area of Palermo, the center of government, progress was slower; corruption had a much stronger hold. For centuries the seat of foreign governments, Palermo had been the hub of patronage needed to placate its endless parade of rulers. Most of the rich landowners lived there, as well as lawyers and fixers who had cajoled endlessly and enriched themselves dealing with the aristocratic world. The task of purging and amending was not simple.

Although parliamentary inquiries were undertaken in an attempt to expose the many woes of the island, despite setbacks, Sicilians themselves were succeeding where politics had failed to improve their fate. Tragically, the promising momentum of Sicily's grass-roots burgeoning was halted by a calamitous earthquake which brought total devastation to Messina in 1908. In addition the Piedmont government's new foreign policy ended any further progress. Italy's conquest of Libya and Eritrea in 1911 devoured the few financial resources which might otherwise have been applied to solving the problems of the South, as Italy's dream of conquest developed into a far too costly mirage.

The calamitous earthquake of 1908 and Italy's imperialistic thrust in North Africa were quickly followed by the disastrous advent of World War I. Despite Italy's continued lack of compassion for the island's despair, Sicilians answered the call to arms *en masse* with valiant soldiers, 50,000 of whom gave their lives and 9,331 of whom were decorated for valor, including 25 who received gold medals of honor.[106]

Sicily's best statesmen made invaluable contributions to their country and to the war effort: Marchese Antonino Sangiuliano, who, as foreign minister, guided the development of the conflict, and Vittorio Emanuele Orlando who, as prime minister, guided Italy to final victory. The war was, however, a huge economic blow for the island as the Sicilian market was closed and Sicily was cut out of trade, deprived of raw materials, and experienced a worsening, deadly isolation. Consequently poverty increased, technology stagnated, and the road and bridge crises worsened.

With the war finally over and Italy among the victors, soldiers returned home with new ambitions and greater expectations for themselves and their families; they found instead a destitute land that offered very little. As an incentive to military service, soldiers had been promised land, but as they returned home they found inflation and strong resistance to land reform. Great unrest followed. The result, by 1919 and 1920, was a takeover of large tracts of land by soldiers and peasants, some now waving the red flag of Communism. Legislators were quick to realize the necessity to legitimize these spontaneous land possessions and the division of some large estates was accomplished.[107]

Reforms were becoming effective after the island's wartime isolation, but the political unrest, which was uprooting the rest of Europe, began to envelop the island too. Fascism was creating a dangerous moment. In Sicily, as in the rest of Italy after World War I, the "old elite" felt menaced by radical groups. Latifondisti felt threatened by the loss of their lands. Therefore, although Sicily had been the least Fascist region of Italy, many members of the establishment adapted to the new regime, if only superficially, in their quest for support against unrest and social progress. Mussolini's help was needed by *latifondisti* to block agrarian reform; sulphur-mine owners looked to him to block the nationalization of mines and crush unions that were opposing salary reductions; local businessmen had little reason to oppose the new regime; among intellectuals, including the author, Giovanni

Verga and the Nobel Laureate, Luigi Pirandello, there was only contempt for a parliament in Rome that had succeeded in doing almost nothing for Sicily in 60 years.[108]

Fascism had to grapple with the traditional distrust by Sicilians towards any central government in power. However, after Benito Mussolini visited the island as Italy's prime minister in 1924, and later, in 1937, when he proclaimed Sicily "the geographic center of the Fascist Empire," they deluded themselves that he would efficiently and definitively offer a solution for age-old problems. Some were resolved and many were in the process of solution during the Fascist presence on the island. Cesare Mori, Fascist chief of police, struggled vigorously to eliminate the Mafia and had notable success, but in the long run his was only a temporary cure since mafiosi reorganized their ranks as they were called upon to collaborate with Lucky Luciano and the Allied command prior to the Allied landing in Sicily.

Before the onset of World War II any Fascist projects for agrarian or industrial reform were quickly interrupted and sacrificed to the financial exigencies of Fascist imperialism in Ethiopia. The onset of World War II was followed by a long period of acute deprivation, violent bombardment of urban centers, and military defeats on the island. The Fascist regime was eliminated with the Allied landing in Sicily, in July of 1943.

The End of Fascism: Reentry of Mafia

In May of 1943, the commander of the Italian 6th Army urged Sicilians to resist the invasion with these words, ".....fraternally united, you, proud Sicilians, and we military Italians and Germans....will demonstrate to the enemy that no one will pass through here." Sicily's reaction was less than enthusiastic since very little was felt for a war imposed by Fascim and fought against England and the United States, both traditional friends of Sicily. Suffice it to mention the millions of Sicilian immigrants living in the United States and the large number of Sicilian Americans who were part of the Allied invasion. Subtle propoganda favoring the Allies, propagated by mafiosi active again after Lucky Luciano's intervention, added to Sicilian acceptance of the Allied landing in July, 1943.[109]

As early as 1941, the U.S. Navy sought the help of Lucky Luciano, who was serving time in prison, to assist in the detection of U.S. based subversives on the New York waterfront, who were supplying vital information to the enemy and facilitating the attack and destruction of as many as 150 merchant marine ships as they approached U.S. territorial waters. Navy agents were first supplied with I.D. cards from Joe Lanza, also a gangster, and then from the more powerful Luciano, allowing them to work as laborers up and down the waterfront searching for enemy agents. "Operation Underworld" spread its wings. U.S. agents now got other jobs, until then closed to them, so they could observe and gather information which would lead them to groups sympathetic to the Axis. A sharp drop in the attack and destruction of ships occurred with the collaboration of Luciano with the military. (Thomas Dewey had made the capture of the gangster his mission and in 1936 had him sent to a high security prison where he was kept in almost complete isolation. In 1941 he saw his prisoner approached by the military and later transferred to the Great Meadow facility near Albany. Luciano had agreed to use his influence to help the war effort. His life became comfortable and the prison guest list included his lawyer and his friends, Meyer Lansky, Frank Costello, Joe Adonis, Bugsy Siegel and others).

As the Allied command prepared its attack on Sicily, Luciano induced mafiosi, some of whom had once lived in America, to gather information needed by the Allies and help prepare some of the groundwork for their assault. Positioned in Tunisia, the Allied command received data describing locations of land mines on Sicilian beaches, information which had been given to mafiosi by local fisherman. Army Corps engineers then arrived to deactivate the mines, and the assault on the island began.

Sicily's liberation on July 28, 1943 was followed by the formation of the MIS (Movement for the Independence of Sicily), with its own yellow and red flag with the symbol of the Trinacria (a head with three legs)at its center. By 1944 the movement had 480,000 adherents. Some encouragement came from the Allies who had thoughts of creating another Malta. Another proposal was union with the U.S.A. The Sicilians truly believed in the possibility of a plebiscite under international control which would assure the island peace and liberty. The hymn of Bellini's "Puritani" became the MIS hymn of liberation with modified lyrics:

Contro tiranni italici	"Against Italic tyrants
noi lotterem da forti;	Fight we must with all our might;
meglio affrontar la morte	Better to welcome Death
gridando libertà!	With shouts of Liberty!"

Sicilians returned to their dialect with:

Nun vulemu sfruttaturi,	"We are tired of exploiters
nun vulemu cchiu' tiranni;	we are tired too of tyrants;
lu distinu nostru e' granni	our true destiny is grander
nni la paci e l'onestà.	blessed with peace and honesty.
La bannera siciliana	Our beloved Sicilian banner
è lu signu di l'onuri,	is the symbol of our honor,
è lu focu di l'amuri	it's the fire of our love
ppi la nostra libbirta'.	For our dream of liberty."[110]

The dream ended with the rapid collapse of Germany in May, 1945. This reduced the Anglo-American political incentive to sustain a separatist movement in Sicily, which would have weakened Italy's position in the future framework of NATO. In October, 1945, the Italian government dealt a serious blow to the MIS by occupying its headquarters in the main centers of Sicily and arresting and confining to the island of Ponza its three principal leaders, the honorable Andrea Finocchiaro Aprile, Antonino Varvaro Esq. of Palermo, and Francesco Restuccia Esq. of Messina. The internal weakness of the MIS, its lack of solidarity and unity of action, also contributed to the failure of Sicily's movement for independence. Undoubtedly, the Movement did serve as a catalyst, together with terrorist threats by EVIS (Volunteer Army for the Independence of Sicily), to highlight the Sicilian question and deserves credit for having energized and accelerated the solution of the problem of autonomy.

The central government granted Sicily extensive regional autonomy in May of 1946. The first elections after the granting of regional government saw a sharp drop in separatist votes and a sharp increase in Communist and Socialist strength. The "old elite" rallied around the Christian Democratic party which represented the political center. The criminal element, newly returned to the island, supported the Right. In the 1948 election the Christian Democrats doubled their representation in Parliament and remained the majority party.

In reparation for injustices done to Sicily in 86 years of Italian central government, a cash fund drawn from local Sicilian taxes was established and deposited annually with the Sicilian region. It was finally understood that the problem of autonomy should not be confused with Italian regional problems in general, since they differed in aims, attitudes, and origin.[111]

The Sicilian Parliament, the oldest in Europe, whose activity had ended with the revolution of 1848, was reconvened in Palermo on May 20, 1947.

The Mafia, almost eliminated during Fascism, became powerful as the regional government established itself. During the interim period between war and peace in Sicily, under the military governorship of Charles Poletti (former lieutenant governor of New York), many mafiosi were released from prison, and, posing as anti-Fascists, were installed in the new administration, filling influential positions vacated by ousted Fascists. Don Calogero Vizzini, one of the best known of the surviving Mafia leaders who had been jailed by Mussolini, was named mayor of Villalba, a strategic town in the Allied passage through the island. His underlings became mayors of surrounding towns. Until his death in 1954, he and his associates gained enormous power through kinship and old and new techniques of banditry and terrorism. Giuseppe Genco Russo, another reputed Mafia leader, newly returned, was also appointed mayor of his town, Mussomeli.[112]

"Project Military and the Underworld" stated that "The Allies had put Mafiosi back in business after Mussolini had sent them to jail and exile. When the Allies left Sicily for the mainland in August of 1943 they left dons in charge, and when the Allies claimed victory over the Axis, the mafia also had a big win in large part because of the Allied decision to put them back in power.

One conclusion arrived at by Dennis Mack Smith concerning the effect of Charles Poletti's actions in Sicily was that "the Americans in 1943 had deliberately reintroduced the Sicilian Mafia as a *ruse de guerre* and given it effective power over large areas of Sicilian society." Once again

Palermo, the main source of official permits and government contracts, became the center of this newly returned and more-than-ever menacing criminal element.

(Mafiosi rarely acted as an organization ,but events of post-World War II united them. They initially supported separatism as an organization and their subsequent violent reaction against peasant unrest resulted in united collaboration with the Christian Democratic party. The series of homicides of union leaders all pointed to a criminal society with a common interest in this given point in Sicilian history. Threatened by agitation for reform, latifondisti *appointed countless* mafiosi *as* gabellotti *whose responsibility it became to rescue the land from peasants. Weakened by Fascism's strong government,* mafiosi *welcomed the restoration of a democratic system which empowered them to influence municipal and parliamentary elections. Parties of the left were opposed and the conservative Christian Democratic Party was supported..*

As early as 1892-1894, when peasants hoped to attain fair land-leasing contracts through collective bargaining, their demonstrations were halted by government intervention. After 1918, the same attempts at collective bargaining by peasants were repeated. The government had to be more conciliatory to its ex-soldiers, so latifondisti *and* gabellotti *had to resort to their subculture of criminals to defend their interests. In 1920 alone, four union leaders were killed. After 1943 the landless peasants asked not only for improved leasing contracts but also for land distribution, and some peasants spontaneously took possession of unfarmed land. In the war against organized peasants and cooperatives, unions, and leftist parties, the usual terrorist methods were used: intimidations and assassinations. Between 1945 and 1965 forty-one leaders of the peasant movement were assassinated. The threat of violence was quickly back in control when* latifondisti, *with the support of Charles Poletti, the military governor, appointed well-known* mafiosi *as their* gabellotti *to intimidate and maintain a* status quo.)[114]

By the end of WWII, the Mafia was no longer rural but had become involved in urban activity. Real estate speculations, collusive attainment of public works contracts, and the drug trade became big business. Threatened with industrialization and better-educated workers, mafiosi had to be more forceful. Industrialists, fearful of exposure to protection rackets, hesitated to build factories in and around Palermo. The worst phase began in 1956 with the struggle for control of the area's food markets. Criminal interference with water supply and levies on transport and marketing continued to affect lemon and orange prices; so did a campaign against the use of refrigeration processes which would have spread sales more evenly through the year.[115]

Centuries of Corrupt Foreign Rule: The Mafia Nurtured

Sicily's deadly criminal subculture was spawned in the chaos of foreign misrule rife with suffocating abuses and evil complicity. Foreign aristocrats were rewarded with gifts of vast Sicilian estates by their king for allegiance and collaboration in return. They felt very little or no loyalty to Sicily. Power struggles developed with rival Sicilian *latifondisti.*Both groups became economically and socially abusive and subsequently created their own spheres of influence. Aristocrats were assisted by *gabellotti* and their henchmen who kept the peasants hungry and subjugated. As they did so, *gabellotti* also strengthened their own power and carved out their own pernicious control over townspeople and peasants. A hierarchy of criminal exploitation emerged as a law unto itself with the tacit consent of *latifondisti* and incumbent rulers who had little concern for the welfare of the island and its people.

The Bourbon government also failed to guarantee a truly effective protection of citizens and property, just as the subsequent Italian government failed. Amidst the chaos and criminal exploitation, paradoxically, kinship assistance was able to thrive. Squads organized by "men of respect," were used to keep control in times of critical peasant revolt.This was true as early as 1820, 1848, and 1866 during political and peasant uprisings. Their aim was to maintain the *status quo*.[116]

Increase in population without land created excess manpower. *Latifondisti* and their *gabellotti* became the masters of the sharecropper and day laborer who were selected for work, not on an impersonal market, but by recommendation from a "person of respect." The *gabellotto*, as overseer of the land for the landowner, and his henchmen assumed more and more control as they became the extended hand of the landowner. The *gabellotto* was, in most cases, a peasant or small cattle dealer who had become a small property owner, who through extortions had succeeded in elevating himself from the masses and gaining some wealth.

This emerging property-owner-*gabellotto* morphed into the mafioso. Having made his profit by exploiting the tenant and the day laborer, the *gabellotto* began to diminish his obligations towards the *latifondista*. The absentee *latifondista*, always in need of money, often, of necessity, sold land to him or handed over the real power of the land to him, and in transferring power, placed him in a position of influence as a "man of respect." The mafioso, usually of humble origin, had succeeded with his racketeering to rise somewhere between the *gabellotto* and the *latifondista*. Vito Cascio Ferro was the son of an illiterate peasant. Calogero Vizzini was a day laborer whose father was also a peasant. Giuseppe Genco Russo, who after World War II became a man of great power, was a shepherd as a young man.

The powerful facade that the "man of respect" created for himself became the personification of manhood to a mass of peasants subjected for centuries to daily humiliations without recourse. Although known for his strength, the "man of respect" showed humility in his approach to solutions. He protected, mediated, organized, and advised. If eliminating someone for the general good became necessary, he acted. He made many altruistic gestures. His position was legitimized by the masses who revered him as their hero, protector, and compatriot, while they deluded themselves that the mafioso was there for them.

As he acquired power and wealth his quest for respectability began. First he created his own "soldiers" who did violence for him. Second, he made contact with socially and economically useful people — the wealthy, *latifondisti*, priests — who introduced him to administrators of government and justice. As he worked at legalizing his position, he avoided direct contact with lawbreakers and, with his newly attained respectability, he associated with police officials, mayors, members of the judiciary, and government and elected officials.[117]

Just as the Piedmontese government jailed political and social activists, linking them to common criminals and conveniently labelling all of them "mafiosi," the same term was applied to those reactive immigrants and sons of immigrants in the U.S.A. who were looking for work and found, instead, unfair labor and union practices which barred them from access. For some of the poor and uneducated and the politically disillusioned it soon became evident that social and political protest, anarchy, and crime were the only solutions to poverty and the iniquities of their new society. The socialist unrest among many Sicilian laborers who were denied jobs and entry into the better unions resulted in many arrests, and the Mafia myth expanded. "Mafia" became a convenient term to apply to all those Italian immigrants and sons of immigrants who caused discomfort — economic, political or criminal — to the Establishment.

Italians who gained notoriety as criminals in America either were born here or came as young children. They were introduced to the violence of American ethnic gang warfare on the city streets. Some of the young immigrants or first generation Italian Americans without work, skills, moral fortitude, or education turned to the streets. As early as the 1890s, the Neapolitan, Paolo Vaccarelli, leader of the Five Points gang, led 1500 men — Jewish, Irish, and Italian. Monk Eastman, son of a Jewish restaurateur was his chief rival.[118] His gang was not Mafia since Vaccarelli was Neapolitan and his gang members came from several ethnic groups.

Frank Costello, born Francesco Castiglia in the province of Calabria, came to America as a young boy. He roamed the streets of East Harlem with Irish and Jewish hoodlums. Later, he and his partner, Henry Horowitz, led a criminal organization. During prohibition Costello dominated the liquor business in the Northeast. Many in the Coast Guard and politics were in his pay.[119]

Amidst all these activities, he did not belong to any "family." Costello was not Sicilian. His associates were Jewish, Irish, Italian, and American. It was a polyethnic criminal organization, not Mafia.

Al Capone was born in Brooklyn in 1899, the son of a barber from Naples. He received his education in neighborhoods near the Brooklyn Navy Yard, where the newly arrived Italians challenged the Irish gangs who felt their dock jobs were threatened, and in Williamsburg, where the Jews were hostile to all strangers. Capone did not belong to any "family." His criminal organization consisted of close to one thousand men from every ethnic group in New York and Chicago.[120]

This most notorious "mafioso" of all, whose violent image has been perpetuated by journalism and the film and television industries, was not a mafioso since Capone's criminal organization consisted of members of many ethnic groups and Capone was not a Sicilian.

Joseph Bonanno came to America as a child of three with his parents to settle in Brooklyn. He attended school here until the second grade when the family returned to Sicily. He had difficulty adjusting since he was more American than Sicilian. If he had not been expelled from school for refusing to wear the Fascist black shirt as a sign of support for the Fascist regime, he probably would not have returned to America. But in 1924 he did return and elbowed his way into the flourishing bootlegging business. His was another of many criminal organizations. Joe Rosselli was born in Esteria, Italy, Joseph Gallo was born in Brooklyn. Paul Ricca was born in Naples. Joe Valachi was born in New York of Neapolitan parents. He was a confessed murderer whose questionable testimony included the term *cosa nostra* which the media quickly adopted as a synonym for Mafia.[121]

The ambiguities concerning Lucky Luciano's collaboration with the U.S. Military in the detection of enemy agents on the N.Y. waterfront and the preparation of Sicily for the Allied invasion seem to be surfacing with certainty now. Born in Sicily, he was brought to America as a boy of 10. His education came from the streets of New York. His mentor was Arnold Rothstein and his cohorts were Bugsy Siegel, Meyer Lansky, Louis Lepke, and George Uffner. Very few genuine Mafiosi seemed to be present among this gang of criminals. According to "Any Means to an End: Project Military and the Underworld" viewed on the History channel in December, 1997, Lucky Luciano cooperated with the U.S. Military in repositioning the exiled Mafia for its role in the preparation of Sicily before and during the Allied landing. Also in question is the behavior of Thomas Dewey who boosted his political career through publicity he attained as a criminal prosecutor in New York when he went after Luciano and his gang. The gangmembers included Lucky Luciano, Abe Wahrman, David Marcus, Thomas Pennocchio, and Jack Ellenstein. Luciano was convicted of running a prostitution ring and was given the unusually harsh sentence of thirty to fifty years in prison. Dewey later sent the prostitutes who testified that Luciano was the ringleader to France, all expenses paid.[122] In 1945 Luciano's lawyer asked that he be set free, pointing out his contribution to the war effort. Ironically, Dewey, the man who had put Luciano in prison, now, as governor, had the power and will to commute his sentence. The parole board supported Dewey's decision and Luciano was deported to Italy. Dewey was plagued for the rest of his days by the accusation that he had been bribed to commute Luciano's sentence since the Navy denied any collaboration with the gangster.

1944: Regional Autonomy: The Dream and The Reality

The Italian government agreed to grant regional autonomy to Sicily in 1944, putting an end to the turmoil of separatist and extremist unrest. This semi-autonomous regional government did not bring all the advantages hoped for, but bigger and more beneficial changes in the economy occurred than any that had resulted since the union with Italy in 1861. Furthermore, besides a special grant of money to the region as reparation for past injustices, Rome increased its expenditure on Sicilian roads and other public works. Farm laborers had a vote under the new law of universal suffrage, and politicians, at last, became interested in them.

Despite changes in the pattern of landownership over the previous forty years, in 1946 probably half the agricultural area of Sicily continued to be owned by one per cent of the population. After WW II, two decrees, one by a Communist minister, the other by a Christian Democrat, were aimed at creating cooperatives and making landowners grant more equitable contracts of tenure.

A special department of the regional government saw to it that landowners farmed productively. Any *latifondo* larger than 500 acres where proprietors failed to carry out improvements faced expropriation. This threat had positive results. Another half million acres were broken up into small and medium holdings over the next fifteen years.[123] The abolition of the *latifondo* was finally written into the Italian Constitution.

By 1960 emigration was again one of Sicily's and southern Italy's big problems. Many rich Sicilians continued to live on the mainland and much income derived from Sicily continued to be spent outside the island. A great many of the best scholars, administrators, and creative minds also continued to leave for the North.[124]

A more serious kind of emigration, especially from 1955-60, concerned citizens of the poorer agricultural areas. Sicilians and other southern Italians discovered that a job in the North could earn, in one month, as much as could be earned in a year back home. Some half million, from a population of now nearly five million, left Sicily in ten years. Obviously the island's economy was not developing fast enough to satisfy more wordly demands and to absorb the annual increase in population. Once again emigration helped relieve the pressure and increase the wages of those who remained. Money was once again sent back by emigrants to their families at home. Paradoxically, this emigration favored industries of the North, for whom the valuable foreign bills, received in Rome's banks, paid for the acquisition of raw materials.125

After a promising beginning, politics and the thoughtless administration of public money shook the Sicilian's faith in a florid future. The problem, according to Prof. Santo Correnti, was that as long as the island had a firm concept of autonomy, and its regional deputies favored Sicily's interests above those of the party, everything went well, but inefficient and sometimes self-serving regional bureaucrats wasted public money.[126]

Frequently, large national companies took advantage of generous government subsidies and installed industrial plants which remained outside the economy of the island, and profits derived from these "cathedrals in the desert" went to the North.127 Although since 1954, 90% of petroleum extracted in Italy has come from oil wells in Ragusa and Gela and is directly refined in Gela, Augusta, and Milazzo, Sicily, Sicilians are not favored by any reduction of government taxes placed on that Sicilian gasoline. At the same time, in Val d'Aosta, in northwest Italy, where no oil is extracted or refined, citizens benefit from notable tax exemptions on gas! Sicily must persuade the central government to correct this discrimination. Prof. Correnti speaks of "the problem of Class A Italians who enjoy unjustified privileges and Class B Italians upon whom unjustified burdens are placed."128

At meetings of the European common market, Italian delegates pushed rice from Val Padana and not oranges from Sicily; in fact, in the markets around Italy large quantities of oranges from Israel and Spain were sold. The government denied Sicily fair treatment: capital investments were frequently rerouted from Sicily to other regions, such as the ironworks promised to Sicily and then shifted to Calabria. In 1958 the American company, Sverdrup and Parcel of St. Louis, Missouri, builders of the Verrazzano Narrows bridge, offered to construct a suspension bridge across the strait of Messina without capital investment from Italy, asking only toll revenue for a certain number of years. The Italian government declined the proposal and the reason has remained obscure. Furthermore, the Italian government allows casinos to exist in San Remo, Campione, Saint Vincent, and Venice. According to Prof. Correnti, "it seems that only with the Sicilian casino does the government remember that gambling is immoral."129 The casino in Taormina was not allowed to open.

Difficulties notwithstanding, many positive achievements have brought satisfaction. The economy, which had improved very little between 1861 and 1950, now carries a substantial annual growth rate. Many problems of the island have been under scrutiny more seriously and expertly than ever before and with resources never available to previous generations. The development of North Africa and the existence of the European Common Market have been creating new economic possibilities.

Local legislation granted tax advantages to outside capital. Within 15 years the number of corporations rose from 218 to 1,576. Laws favorable to prospectors encouraged foreign companies to join in the search for oil. In 1953, the Gulf Oil Company struck oil near Ragusa and the first refinery was built in Augusta with pipelines linking it to Ragusa. When the Italian company, ENI, discovered another field in the sea off Gela, Sicily became responsible for nearly the whole of a considerable Italian oil industry. Four refineries were built to deal with this and with great quantities of imported crude oil from Russia, the Near East, and Libya. A pipeline was built to connect Gela to Gagliano where an important discovery of methane gas opened up the possibility of developing Enna, one of the poorest provinces of Sicily. Other pipelines were built connecting other key points on the island, and at last Sicily was attaining the cheap power necessary to make industrialization possible and free itself from isolation.[130]

A thermoelectric plant, a cement works, factories producing fertilizers, plastics, and other petrochemicals emerged. The ancient town of Gela changed more in five years than in the previous thousand. For the first time, a proper port was built on the south coast, and a three-mile jetty was built out to an island terminal where ships could load. The number of tractors used in agriculture was still under a thou-sand at the end of Mussolini's regime; by 1955 it was five times as many, and by 1962 twice as many again. Augusta emerged after the war as the busiest Sicilian

port; a century earlier it had been almost empty. By 1964 it led Venice and Naples for tonnage handled, after which it surpassed Genoa to become the foremost port in Italy. With rapid growth in industry, burdensome ecological problems emerged demanding attention and solution.

A shift towards a greater variety of crops has been beneficial. Agricultural experts encouraged cultivation of grapes and tomatoes. The lemon and orange harvest have come to exceed that of any other region in Italy. There has been a twofold increase in the potato crop and a fivefold increase in the artichoke crop. One eighth of Italy's olive oil is produced in Sicily. Flax and cotton have become increasingly important. About one fourth of Italy's fishing boats sail from Sicilian ports. Wine production has been encouraged and great strides have been made. Sicily has the most vineyards of any region, marked by an extraordinary density of vines in Trapani province and much of Agrigento. Its production of wine, second only to the Apulia region, proudly boasts many excellent DOC reds and whites, such as Etna

Bianco DOC, Alcamo DOC, Cerasuolo di Vittoria DOC, Malvasia di Lipari DOC, and Moscato di Pantelleria DOC.[132]

The island's road system has been vastly improved by ultra-modern superhighways crisscrossing most of the island and creating accessibility to even the most remote sections. Even the poorest have been given the possibility of knowing their island, its people, and its treasures. Isolation has been further removed as televisions, telephones, and automobiles have become part of every household.

Sicilians continue striving against the Mafia as they join together cooperating to rid their island of this criminal parasite. Imbued with a new sense of unity and pride, Sicily's fight against crime has been significant. Since the end of World War II the Mafia has become brutally violent in its war against prosecutors and investigations. Perhaps at the root of this excessive cruelty lies the knowledge that much of its traditional influence has been lost and that its demise may be imminent. Perhaps, after its almost complete elimination by the Fascist regime, excessive violence was its way of regaining control. Sicilians, strengthened by their pride in self-government, repudiated organized crime's association with drugs and prostitution. Improved schools, 97% literacy, greater ease of movement inside Sicily, and the emancipation of women all have helped to threaten Mafia power. A strong thrust comes from organizations of women, including wives of officials killed by the Mafia, who firmly support the crusade against criminality in Sicily. They have taken their cause to the people, to schools, and into public squares. Silent anti-Mafia demonstrations are not infrequent sights in the larger public squares of major Sicilian cities. "The wall of silence" has been broken as witnesses give testimony to "their" judiciary. The avowed anti-Mafia former mayor, Emanuele Orlando, elected by landslide vote in Palermo, initiated many reforms and magnificent restorations in the city.

The Mafia has always counted on fear. Recently, however, businesses have been openly defying the Mafia by signing onto a Web site called "Addiopizzo" (Goodbye Protection Money) which is succeeding in bringing together businesses on the island that are resisting extortion.

Confindustria, the industrialists' lobby, has also supported the movement by attempting to prevent their members from paying protection money. Interestingly, authorities who are intensifying pressure on business owners, aggressively prosecute those who refuse to testify against the Mafia in clear cut cases of extortion. Under Italian law, a business man who denies paying up despite flagrant evidence can be charged with "aiding and abetting" organized crime activities. Attitude of many is that it is a greater risk for them to pay than not to pay.

A former Mafia boss, fearing that excessive greed and violence would draw fierce police reaction, since 1993, followed a "low profile" towards extortion tactics accepting smaller protection payments but making everyone pay. Under new leadership, the low profile was dispensed with. According to Piero Grasso, the former Palermo prosecutor, now Italy's national anti-Mafia prosecutor based in Rome, under the new boss shake downs have been more than doubled. A rash of arson attacks on businesses apparently reflected the determination of the criminals to extort.

A hopeful note is that the tough strategy seems to have backfired. The more ruthless the Mafia action became, the more their victims resisted.

The latest Mafia boss was arrested in November, 2007. Police found, with his arrest, a list of hundreds of names of those who had paid "pizzo" and how the money was divided up. This will, inevitably lead to further investigations and purging.

CONCLUSION

The course of Sicilian history has been changed significantly. The granting of regional autonomy and the gift of "patria" to the people has opened a world of aspirations. Citizens maturing in an ambience of freedom and democracy have become inspired to work together with pride and a new consciousness for the common good. Exploitation and corruption are confronted, and concentrated efforts for reform are made. Much still needs to be accomplished, but time has been short. Northern Italian newspapers have written that "Sicily undoubtedly has progressed greatly with regional autonomy, having achieved goals which 20 years ago seemed unachievable," and that "Sicily in 15 years of regional autonomy had realized stupefying progress." (*Oggi*, July 20, 1961.)

Sicilians must fully become aware of and search for solutions to the many problems that persist on their island. To a great extent they have undertaken the task. On the other hand, damage done by the central government towards the region also has been grave. There is still a long road with many misconceptions that must be clarified before an effective spiritual unity among all Italians is to be achieved.

Although in 1958 the Italian government failed to approve the construction of a bridge spanning the strait of Messina, which would join the island and the mainland, Sicily independently undertook the challenge. During the term of Prof. Provenzano, the then president of the region of Sicily, his administration became involved in exciting collaboration with the region of Calabria to construct that bridge. Architectural plans were completed, and the year 2006 was the estimated date of completion. The project, a superb single-span suspension bridge, blended the most modern Italian scientific technology with all the aesthetic grace that art and modern architecture has to offer.[133]

This project of staggering proportions has not yet come to fruition. Three avenues of funding were under consideration: the first favored by the two regions directly involved opened the bidding to the international financial community; in the second plan the Italian government would finance and supervise construction of the bridge; in the third, the European Union would become involved.

Unfortunately, planning has been delayed and a date for project completion is not available.

Freedom and self-determination have allowed Sicilians to re-evalute the immense wealth of their historical and architectural patrimony. Newly nurtured pride and social conscience have sounded the alarm for action to preserve the island's treasures, and collaboration is in progress throughout

Sicily as museums, churches, historical sites, and gardens are being painstakingly restored.

The Cultural Center of Federico II opened its doors to the public in 1995 in Menfi, an industrious town of 15,000 inhabitants on the southern coast of Sicily between Agrigento and Selinunte. The Institute's aim, found in its brochure, "Esposizione Permanente" is "not only to disseminate scientific and humanistic culture, but also to satisfy the desire for knowledge, to encourage a spirit of tolerance, and to coordinate all the initiatives that contribute to the cultural and civil growth of a territory." The Institute is enriched by a modern scholastic video cassette library, computer systems with access to the National Library System and the Internet, and a highly specialized interdisciplinary library which offers ample possibility for anyone from town or elsewhere, to do intensive professional research. The second floor of the Institute houses two permanent exhibits, archeology and malacology, which are the corner stones for a future civic museum. The malacology exhibit, circa 6,000 magnificent seashells gathered from around the world, is documented and displayed with total professionalism. About this exhibit, donated by Vanna Rotolo Lombardo, a native of Menfi, a "notably didactic aim" is put forth. "By bringing to the viewers the incredible diversity and beauty of some of our planet's life-forms, it is hoped that a deep appreciation of the splendor, ingeniousness, and mystery of Nature will be encouraged, particularly in this epoch in which constant attack on our natural habitat is damaging its patrimony dangerously."

In Palermo, a city of almost one million inhabitants, common citizens, professionals, and officials have responded quickly to the alarm, and restoration of an abandoned historical quarter of the city, La Kalsa has been undertaken. Many offered their professional expertise gratuitously to the dynamic and farsighted mayor, LeoLuca Orlando, and his council, and the city became involved and fascinated by the project. At the inauguration ceremony after completion of the first stage of restoration, it was with great enthusiasm and pride that both mayor and citizens applauded the splendid achievement. The first stage focused on a section called *Lo Spasimo* (spasm or pain) is composed of the municipal warehouses, an adjoining hospital and a 15th century church.[134]

Lo Spasimo, now restored to its original splendor, is used as a cultural center where citizens come to enjoy concerts, drama, and lectures. The gardens, beautifully renovated, offer access to the church and to the many newly restored cobblestone streets where pedestrians, as they meander through the area, seem to step into a past resplendent in the beauty of its revived townhouses. Further on, in one of the small, revitalized piazzas, sidewalk cafes and restaurants invite the passersby to rest and enjoy a fine meal. The return of *Lo Spasimo* to citizens of Palermo has in fact produced an influx of social activity into an urban area almost completely unknown to the majority of citizens and especially to the youth who grew up in the midst of poorly planned real estate speculation in the 1970s. Until a few years ago, it was unthinkable to imagine young couples walking in that area; it was unthinkable to plan a meeting with friends in the heart of the old city, or to attend a concert or see an art exhibit there.

Another major project of restoration in *La Kalsa* at Piazza Maggione is underway. In addition to the laborious work on the infrastructure and buildings, a newly acquired sensitivity at the planning level is giving careful consideration to the inclusion of collective cultural activities which will appeal to the generations, but with a considered emphasis on cultural interests of the young.

Today, thanks to this interaction of citizens and a growing professionalism and sensitivity in city halls throughout the island, a cultural endeavor has been initiated which seems to be unstoppable.

Palermo's historical center has become an open workshop where nothing is built without a plan, and where the latest techniques are used to restore and make the invaluable treasures of Sicily's legacy resplendent again. In Menfi, the Institute "hopes to endow to all citizens a site for research and a meeting place for the intellectual, civil, and moral progress of her population."

Fulfillment of political, economical, and social potentials now seem to be within the grasp of these resilient survivors who finally have the opportunity, as free and united citizens, to work in concert towards that aim. Through the centuries this survivor, whose character was formed in the crucible of his tumultuous history, used his creative intelligence, his diligent nature, his courage, and his ironic acceptance of a malign fate to endure and at last to overcome. His genuine love of family, instinctive courtesy, and generous hospitality made his tortured life tolerable. His humorous irony and intelligence were recognized as early as the first century B.C. by Cicero who defines the Sicilian as intelligent, but suspicious, adding that even if something goes badly for him, he surmounts it with a witty, *ad hoc* remark:

Ringraziamu a Diu pi chiddu chi nni duna,
e a lu re pi chiddu chi nni lassa!

"Let's thank God for what He gives us,
and the king for what he leaves for us!"[135]

as he refers to exploitation suffered at the hands of Bourbon kings. When Sicily was hit with a hail of taxes, including the inheritance tax, the Sicilians bantered that now they had become "parenti du re" ("relatives of the king") since at their death the king inherited from the dead islanders' estates! Johann Von Goethe, in his *Italian Journal,* offers this description of a Palermitan shopkeeper, "Having got into his stride, he went on to poke fun at various examples of police corruption, giving me reassuring proof that man still retains enough sense of humor to mock at what he cannot mend."

Sparse is the documentation espousing the suffering and the heroism of Sicilians as they struggled endlessly to rid their land of oppressors. Nevertheless, one has only to examine the events of the last century to feel the emotional impact of the valiant lives lost, the fierce battles fought, the eternal desire to shape one's own destiny, as Sicilians defied insurmountable odds, with barely more than their hands, to free their cities from Bourbon oppressors in 1820, 1848, and again in 1860.

"Scurra sangu ppi tutta sta terra,	Let blood flow throughout our land,
s'abbruciassi ogni nostra città:	Let all our cities burn:
tutti morti, ma schiavi nissunu	Let all be killed, but none enslaved
di sta 'nfami canagghia di re!"	by this wicked scoundrelof a king!

This battle hymn was sung by rebels as they faced defeat and the destruction of their city by the Bourbon army. (1848 defense of Messina) And again they sang in 1860 as they swelled Garibaldi's *Mille* with 3,000 volunteers who gave the General the strength to go on to victory in a short time.

All'erta tutti ppi lu quattru aprili!	On guard one and all on April 4th!
Sangu ppi sangu nni l'avemu a fari:	We've got to fight blood against blood:
'sta setta impia l'avemu a finiri,	This unholy sect wipe out we must,
la Sicilia l'avemu a libbirari! [136]	and so doing, to Sicily bring liberty!

Their valor during WW I, a war Italy fought alongside American and English allies against Austria and Germany, truly merits praise: 50,000 Sicilian lives lost, 9,331 decorations for valor, 25 of which were gold medals of honor.

It is regrettable that the centuries-old Sicilian struggle, in particular during the last century, has been obscured by tactics to stigmatize all insurrections as Mafia-related when most were legitimate attempts to achieve freedom, to achieve self-government, to achieve viable distribution of land and decent working conditions, attempts to improve a standard of living dangerously spiralling downward.

In his pamphlet *What Makes a Sicilian?* Prof. Gaetano Cipolla of St. John's University writes, "sixteen foreign dominations have left their mark on the Sicilian's soul. Cautious? Suspicious? Yes, indeed! No one has come to Sicily with gifts. They have all come to take something."[137]

He speaks of the Sicilian ego which he says often borders on exaggeration, making him excessive, since he must always see himself as the best. Certainly, the Sicilian's strong love of family is the nucleus of his existence, a characteristic which seems to be universally Italian. He reveres the elderly and the dead. In fact, the Sicilian has "the dead" bring children gifts on "All Souls Day," assuring for them a loving tradition of remembrance even by the children in the family. Prof. Cipolla introduces the interesting thought that "the natural excesses of geography and weather are reflected in the character of the Sicilian. In Tomasi di Lampedusa's *Il Gattopardo*, set in 1860, the Prince of Salina summed it up by saying that together with foreign dominations and incongruous violence, the atmosphere, climate and Sicilian landscape were the forces which together shaped the Sicilian soul. The landscape which knows only excesses, the excessive heat for six months of the year, the torrential rains which flood the rivers, drown cattle and men alike, the scarcity of water which must be carried from afar, have all contributed to form a character which remains conditioned by its fate and an overwhelming insularity of soul.[138]

Obviously, a new conditioning has occurred in the last few decades; fate is less malign, and insularity is being erased by universal education, modern communications, mass media, travel, and a greatly improved standard of living.

Perhaps the most eloquent image of the Sicilian character is derived from the courage, determination, selflessness, quest for education, and generosity of spirit which led millions to emigrate, to leave their homes, *not* to *forget* their loved ones, but to enrich the aspirations of those left behind, through the fruit of their labor.

This melting pot of Europe, this resilient and extraordinary people has overcome great hardships for millennia, and now regional autonomy, for which so many sacrificed their lives, has brought that gift of "patria" and the legislative means to fulfill the island's promise.

In 1787 Wolfgang Goethe wrote, "To have seen Italy without having seen Sicily leaves no imprint upon the soul because within Sicily is the key to everything."

BIBLIOGRAPHY

Agliano, Sebastiano. *Questa Sicilia.* Venice: Corbo e Fiore, 1982.

Barbera, Henry. *Medieval Sicily: The First Absolute State.* New York: Legas 1994.

Battaglia, G.G. *La rivoluzione sociale siciliana.* Palermo: David Malato, 1970.

Brea, Bernabò. *Sicily Before the Greeks.* New York: Frederick A. Praeger.

Chierichetti, Sandro. *Capolavori della Sicilia.* Milano: Usmati Editore, 1973.

Correnti, Santo. *Storia di Sicilia come storia.* Catania: Gruppo Editoriale Brancato, 1995.

De Palma, Claudio. *La Magna Grecia.* Rome: Newton Compton, 1980.

Finley, Moses I. *Storia della Sicilia antica.* Roma: Laterza & Figli, 1979.

Finley - Mack Smith - Duggan. *Breve storia della Sicilia.* Rome: Laterza, 1992.

Freeman, E.A. *History of Sicily.* London: Oxford University Press,1891.

Gambino, Richard. *Blood of My Blood.* New York: Doubleday & Co., Inc., 1974.

Hess, Henner. *Mafia.* Rome: Laterza & Sons, 1993.

Hurè, Jean. *Storia della Sicilia.* Palermo: Editore Ri.Si., 1982.

La Rosa, Vincenzo. *Le popolazioni della Sicilia: Sicani, Siculi, Elimi.* Milano: Schewiller, 1989.

Mangione, Jerre & Morreale, Ben. *La Storia: Five Centuries of the Italian American Experience.* New York: Harper Collins Publishers, 1992.

Montanelli, Indro. *Storia dei Greci.* Milano: Rizzoli, 1979.

Natoli, Luigi. *Storia di Sicilia.* Palermo: S.F. Flaccovio, 1989.

Pitrè, Giuseppe. *Usi e costumi: credenze e pregiudizi del popolo siciliano.* Palermo: 1889.

Quatriglio, Giuseppe. *A Thousand Years in Sicily: from the Arabs to the Bourbons.* New York: Legas 1987.

Rivoire, Mario. *Federico II.* Milano: Arnaldo Mondadori, 1969.

Romano, Sergio. *Storia d'Italia dal Risorgimento ai nostri giorni.* Milano: Mondadori, 1977.

Sciascia, Leonardo. *Il giorno della civetta.* Torino: Einaudi, 1961.

Sebilleau, Pierre. *La Sicilia.* Bologna: Cappelli, 1968.

Simeti, Mary Taylor. *On Persephone's Island: A Sicilian Journal.* San Francisco: North Point Press, 1987.

Smith, Denis Mack. *A History of Sicily.* 2 vols. New York: The Viking Press, 1968.

Tomasi di Lampedusa, G. *Il Gattopardo.* Milano: Feltrinelli, 1961.

Notes

1. Brea, Bernabò. *Sicily before the Greeks.* New York: Frederick A. Praeger, p.28.
2. *Ibid.*
3. *Ibid,* p.38.
4. *Ibid.,* p.61.
5. De Palma, Claudio, *La Magna Grecia.* Newton Compton,Rome:1990. p. 24.
6. *Ibid.,* p.26.
7. *Ibid.,* p. 25
8. Natoli, Luigi. *Storia di Sicilia.* Palermo: S.F. Flaccovio, 1989, p.30.
9. Brea. op.cit., p.109.
10. Pantalica facies is subdivided into four periods: 1270B.C. to 1000B.C., identified in the necropoli of North and Northwest Pantalica (Syracuse), 1000 B.C. to 850 B.C., necropoli of Cassibile (Syracuse), 850B.C. to 730B.C., necropoli of South Pantalica and Monte Finocchito near Noto (Syracuse), 730B.C., necropoli of Monte Bubbonia (Caltanisetta, St. Angelo Muxaro-Agrigento, and Licodia Eubea-Catania.
11. La Rosa, *Le popolazioni della Sicilia: Sicani, Siculi, Elimi.,* Schewiller, Milano:1989, p.12.
12..Brea, op.cit., p.167.
13. Sebileau, Pierre. *La Sicilia,* Bologna: Cappelli, p.49. Segesta was founded in 630 B.C. by a mysterious population, the Elymi, who in the course of the preceding millennium had come from the East, from Asia, Phoenicia, or even Troy. Segesta never considered itself a Greek city and defended its original pretext of being Trojan. Thus she was able to flourish in the midst of Carthaginean territory. Simeti, Mary Taylor in *Persephone's Island* says instead that the predominating influence was Greek, not Carthaginean. The Segestans adopted the Greek alphabet to inscribe their pottery, They absorbed Greek culture so well that many marriages were contracted with Greek citizens.
14. The Phoenicians: an ancient semitic people from the Syrian-Palestinian coastline were the founders of Carthage. Evidence has been found of Phoenician infiltration on the west and north coast of Sicily, around 1000 B.C., for the purpose of creating ports of call along the shore. The Phoenicians were linguistically and culturally related to the semitic inland peoples known as Canaanites. They were bold sea-faring people and cunning traders. The Phoenician alphabet was devised in the 2nd millennium B.C. and adapted by the Greeks circa 800 B.C. and was subsequently transmitted to western Europe via Rome.
15. Ionia — an area in the central part of the western coast of Anatolia (western Turkey) where Ionic Greek was spoken. Many Mycenaean Greeks (Crete), who dominated the Aegean by the 13th century B.C., emigrated to Ionia in order to escape the invading Dorians (c.1000 B.C.). Their close contact with the more advanced civilization of the East quickly raised their level of culture.
16. The Dorians were a Greek speaking people who migrated into Greece after 1200B.C. by way of western Jugoslavia. They settled in Crete and in the Peloponnesus which is the southern most oart of the mainland of Greece, a broad peninsula connected to the mainland by the Isthmus of Corinth.
17. Chalcedon, a Greek city on the island of Eubea, the second largest after Crete.
18. Corinth, of Doric origin and Sparta were the chief cities of the Peloponnesus.
19. Megaris, district of ancient Greece on the Isthmus of Corinth; was destroyed by the Visigoths in 395 A.D.

20. Montanelli, Indro. *Storia dei Greci*. Milano: Rizzoli, 1979, p. 384. Gelone ruled after the defeat of a democratic regime which had, in its time, defeated the old, conservative regime. Gelone's intelligence was inversely proprtional to his scruples, while his success was directly proportional to the crimes which resulted in his success.

21. Freeman, E.A. *History of Sicily*. London: Oxford University Press, 1991.

22. Imera was destroyed by the Carthaginians in 409 B.C. and then was to be rebuilt and renamed Termini Imerese which is the name it still has today.

23. Simeti, Mary Taylor. *On Persephone's Island*. San Francisco: North Point Press. 1987, p. 207. Segesta relied on diplomacy for her defense, playing off Carthaginian against Greek and Athenians against Syracusans in their search for allies to support them in their border controversies with Selinunte. In 416 when Selinunte received the support of Syracuse, Segesta called upon the Athenians, on the mainland, for aid. Segesta borrowed all the gold and silver goblets and plates that Erice (another Elymian town) could lend them and set them out with their own gold and silver in order to impress the Athenian delegation. The Athenians were so impressed with Segesta's wealth that it was agreed that they would support Segesta in her war against Selinunte and Syracuse.

24. De Palma, op.cit., p.188.

25. *Ibid.*, p.189.

26. Finley, Moses, I. *Storia della Sicilia*. Roma: Laterza e figli, 1979, p.18.

27. Correnti, Santo. *Storia di Sicilia*. Catania: gruppo Editoriale Brancato, p.19.

28. Finley, op.cit., p. 189.

29. Correnti, op.cit., p.71.

30. Ostrogoths were a Germanic people who settled in the Ukraine. Theodoric the Great became king of Italy (493A.D. - 525 A.D.). Amalasuntha, his daughter, was murdered by her husband who reigned with her. Her allies, the Byzantines soon attacked Italy and Italy fell. As this invasion occurred in Italy, it simultaneously occurred in Sicily.

31. Justinian ruled the Byzantine Empire from 527 to 565 A.D. as one of its greatest emperors. He was born in Scupi (Skopje, Yugoslavia), educated in Constantinople by his uncle Justin, an army officer. Justinian became the power behind the throne when his uncle became emperor as Justin I in 518 A.D. Justinian married Theodora whose support was vital to him; she had qualities of leadership which he lacked, and she succeeded in inspiring him to action.

32. Smith. op. cit., pp. 16-19.Finley-Mack Smith-Duggan. *Breve storia della Sicilia*. Laterza & Figli Spa, Rome, p. 60.

33. *Ibid.*, pp. 77-79.

34. Correnti, op.cit., p.83.

35. Correnti, op.cit., p.82.

36. Smith, Denis Mack. *A History of Sicily*. New York: The Viking Press, 1968, p. 119.

37. Correnti, op.cit., p.87.

38. Smith, op.cit., p.19.

39. In the southwestern section of Palermo lies the Albergheria where the Royal Palace, once inhabited by the officials of the Norman court, can still be found.

40. Correnti, op.cit., p.88.

41. Finley-Mack Smith-Duggan, op.cit., p.90.

42. Correnti, op.cit., p.91.

43. *Ibid.*, p.92.

44. *Ibid.*, p.95.

45. Rivoire, Mario. *Federico II*. Milano: A. Mondadori, 1969, p.17.

46. Communes: self-governing municipalities established in the Middle Ages that guaranteed to its population personal liberty, right to regulate trade and collect taxes, and the right to its own system of justice within its own walls. They emerged in Italy in the 11th century in an attempt to overthrow the rule of the local bishop or feudal magnate.

47. Rivoire. op.cit., pp. 6-8.

48. Finley - Mack Smith - Duggan. op. cit., p. 98.

49. Montanelli. op. cit., p. 52.

50. Rivoire. op.cit., p.79.

51. Finley. op. cit., p. 100.

52. *Ibid.*, p. 104.

53. Sebileau, Pierre. *La Sicilia*. Bologna: Cappelli, 1968, p. 21.

54. Natoli. op.cit., p. 191.

55. *Ibid.*, p. 229.

56. Finley-Mack Smith-Duggan. op. cit., p. 114.

57. *Ibid.*, p. 228.

58. Correnti, op.cit., pp.199-120.

59. *Ibid.*, p.116.

60. *Ibid.*

61. *Ibid.*, p. 137.

62. Finley-Mack Smith-Duggan. op.cit., p. 141.

63. Correnti, op.cit., p.139.

64. Finley-Mack Smith-Duggan, op.cit., p. 155.

65. Correnti, op.cit., p. 149.

66. Finley-Mack Smith-Duggan, op.cit., p. 158.

67. *Ibid.*, p.168.

68. Mack Smith, op.cit., p.248.

69. Correnti, op.cit., p. 174.

70. Natoli, op.cit., p.230.

71. Correnti, op.cit., p. 174.

72. *Ibid*, p. 178.

73. Smith. op. cit,, pp. 278, 292.

74. *Ibid.*, p. 294.

75. Quatriglio, Giuseppe. *A Thousand Years in Sicily: from the Arabs to the Bourbons*. (New York: Legas, 1987, p. 188.

76. Correnti, op.cit., p. 191.

77. Natoli, op.cit., p. 262.

78. *Ibid.*, p. 265.

79. *Ibid.*, p. 269.

80. Correnti, op.cit., p. 214.

81. Mangione, Jerre & Morreale, Ben. *La Storia: Five Hundred Years of the Italian American Experience*. New York: Harper Collins Publishers, 1992. p. 60.

82. Correnti, op.cit., p. 232.

83. *Ibid.*

84. Francesco Crispi was born in Ribera, Sicily, in 1818 and died in Naples, in 1901. As a youth he was an adherent of Mazzini. He was active in organizing the revolutions

of 1848 and 1860. He was the mind behind Garibaldi's social reforms in Sicily. In 1861 he was elected socialist congressman in the new government. He was arrested by the new government. By 1864 he became a monarchist. As Prime Minister of Italy from 1887-1891 and then again from 1893-1896 he ruled authoritatively and actively set out to abolish socialist sentiment. However, by 1894 he returned to his former political ideals and embraced socialism and irredentism for Sicily.

85. Natoli. op. cit., p. 300.

86. *Ibid.*, p. 307.

87. Mangione & Monrreale, op.cit., p. 60.

88. Correnti, op.cit., p. 246.

89. Natoli. op. cit., p. 309.

90. Mangione & Morreale. op. cit., p. 61.

91. Natoli. op. cit., pp. 309-311.

92. Finley - Mack Smith - Duggan. op. cit., p. 281.

93. *Ibid.*, p. 313.

94. Smith. op. cit., p. 456.

95. *Ibid.*, p. 260.

96. *Ibid.*, p. 255.

97. "Fasci" means "bundles" in Sicilian. The "Fasci" symbolized the bringing together of workers and peasants in a Socialist directed movement. The Fasci became the symbol of working-class unity in Sicily. Mussolini exploited his Socialist roots when he adopted the term years later.

98. Finley - Mack Smith - Duggan. op. cit., p. 291.

99. Correnti, op.cit., p. 267.

100. Finley - Mack Smith - Duggan. op. cit., p.74.

101. Pitrè, Giuseppe. *Usi e Costumi: Credenze e Pregiudizi del Popolo Siciliano.* Palermo: 1889.

102. Members of the Camorra, a Neapolitan criminal association.

103. Gambino. op. cit., p.295.

104. *Ibid.*, p. 291.

105. Finley-Mack Smith-Duggan, op.cit., p. 306.

106. Correnti, op.cit., p.264.

107. Finley-Mac Smith-Duggan, op.cit., p. 309.

108. *Ibid.*, p. 310.

109. Correnti, op.cit., p. 266.

110. *Ibid.*, p. 268.

111. *Ibid.*, p. 277.

112. Hess, Henner. *Mafia.* Rome: Laterza & Figli, 1973, p. 197.

113. "Project Military and the Underworld: Any Means to an End" viewed on the History channel, 12/97.

114. Hess. op. cit., p. 193.

115. Smith. op. cit., p. 534.

116. Hess, op. cit., p. 193.

117. *Ibid.*, pp. 91-105.

118. Mangione & Morreale. op. cit., p. 250.

119. *Ibid.*, p. 258.

120. *Ibid.*, p. 259

121. *Ibid.*, pp. 255-257.124

122. *Ibid.*.

123. Smith. op. cit., p. 532.

124. Brancati and Vittorini among the novelists, Guttuso and Consagra among artists, Quasimodo the Nobel poet, and Pirandello the Nobel dramatist, La Malfa, La Pira, Scelba and Riccardo Lombardi among politicians, names that suggest Sicily's continued contribution of more than her full share to Italian life on the mainland. Those writers who, like Tomaso di Lampedusa and Leonardo Sciascia, remained in Sicily, appeared to be indifferent to worldly success.

125. Correnti, op.cit., p. 279.

126. *Ibid.*, p. 280.

127. *Ibid.*

128. *Ibid.*, p. 293.

129. *Ibid.*, p. 288.

130. Smith, op.cit., pp. 537-538.

131. Finley-Mack Smith-Duggan. op. cit., p. 334.

132. Anderson, Burton. *Wine Atlas of Italy*. Simon & Schuster, New York: 1900, p. 297.

133. The bridge which will be built with highly resistant steel, 90% of which to be produced in Italy, will be 3.3 kms long, will have two steel towers and 12 lanes. The cost is projected at 5 billion dollars. The bridge will greatly change the strategy of Italy towards market in North Africa, and Sicily will have the advantage of functioning as an "aircraft carrier" in the Mediterranean. It will also benefit Sicily's commerce and tourism. Three avenues of funding are under consideration: the first is favored by the two regions directly involved: Sicily and Calabria would undertake the project independently of the Italian government, opening the bidding to the international financial community. Investors would recoup their capital from bridge revenues. Meetings to present the financial project have been arranged in New York. In the second plan the Italian government would fund and supervise the construction of the bridge as a government "super project". In a third scenario the European Union, weighing the valuable strategic position of the bridge, would become involved. It is also possible that all three avenues will merge.

134. The church of Santa Maria dello Spasimo built in 1530, became part of a fortress built to defend the city against attacks by the Turkish armada in 1537; in 1624 a grave epidemic of the plague struck Palermo and Lo Spasimo was used as a *lazzaretto* for the dying; again in 1855 the complex was transformed into a hospice for the poor, terminally ill with contagious diseases; then in the early 1900s it became a warehouse for art equipment. Special thanks to Letizia Palagonia, architect, Palermo, for assistance with the Lo Spasimo text. Special thanks to Federica DeBellis, university student of architecture for further assistance and photographs.

135. Correnti, op. cit. p. 213

136. *Ibid.*, p. 234.

137. Cipolla, *What Makes A Sicilian?*, Legas: 1996, p. 7.

138. Tomasi di Lampedusa, *Il Gattopardo*: Feltrinelli, Milano: 1972, pp. 205-206.

Index of Names and Places

70, 92, 109, 124-5, 127-8
Spaniards, 57, 64-5, 68, 92
Sparta, 21-2, 119
Stentinello (near Syracuse), 14-5, 128
Stesicoro, Siceliot poet, 25
St. Conone, 28
St. Paul, 27
St. Sergio, 28
St. Stefano, 28
Stupinigi, castle, 64
Swabians, 11, 42, 45
Syracuse, 14, 16, 19-4, 27-8, 34
Syria, 14, 115

Tancredi 40
Taormina, 24, 34, 65, 109
Taranto, 22
Tarquinia, 16
Temple of Athena, 27
Teocritus, poet of Syracuse, 24
Teodorico, the Ostrogoth, 31
Thaleia, the goddess, 20
Thebes, 35
Thirty Years War, 58
Thucydides, 18
Timeo of Taormina, historian, 24
Torino, 88
Trafalgar, battle of, 73
Trapani, 13, 47, 54, 65, 82, 110
Treaty of London, 65
Treaty of Utrecht, 63-4
Trojan War, 18
Troy, 19
Tunisia, 35, 38, 67, 98
Turkey, 60, 67, 119
Turks, 58, 60
Tuscany, 15, 54, 129

Uffner, George, mobster, 106
Umbria, 15-6
University, of Catania, 55
University, of Florence, 23
University, of Rome, 25
University, of Genoa, 25

Utrecht, Treaty of, 63-4

Vaccarelli, Paolo, 105
Valachi, Joseph, 106
Vandals, 11, 31, 34
Vanguard, Adm. Nelson's flagship, 71
Venice, 40, 60, 109-10, 118
Verga, Giovanni, 97
Vetulonia, 16
Vienna, Congress of, 74
Vikings, 37
Villanova, 16
Vittorio Amadeo, duke of Savoy, 63
Vittorio Emanuele II, king of Italy, 83, 85, 96, 129
Vizzini, Don Calogero, 100, 104

Waterloo, battle of, 74

Zeno, Emperor, 31
Zeus, 20
Zisa, palace/Palermo, 40

Illustrations

High-stemmed cup, Serra d'Alto style. 4000 B.C. (Courtesy of P.V. Basilea).

Large single-handed cup, Serra d'Alto style (Neolithic Period) 4000 B.C.
(Courtesy of P.V. Basilea).

Single-handed pitcher, Moarda style before Castelluccio. 2000 B.C. (Courtesy of P.V. Basilea).

Castelluccio. Large handle pitcher/jug.1800 B.C. (Courtesy of P.Veneroso).

Ritual cup from Castelluccio (west of Partanna) 1800 B.C. (Courtesy of P.V. Basilea).

Long-stemmed tulip vase. Pantalica south (800 B.C.)

Vases in Castelluccio style from Necropolis. Middle Bronze Period, 2nd millennium B.C. (Courtesy of Museo Archeologico, Palermo).

Various objects in Castelluccio style from Ciavolaro, Ribera. 2nd millennium B.C. (Courtesy of Museo Archeologico, Palermo).

Vase with ;large decorative spiral handles. "Diana Culture" (IV millennium B.C.)

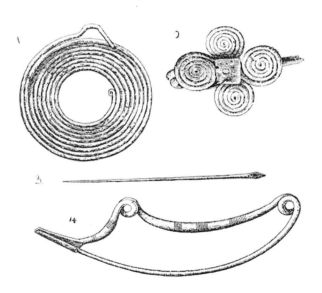

1. Disc-shaped spiral. 2. Cruciform fibula. 3. Needle with eye. 4. Looped fibula with curved pin. Bronzes from Pantalica South Cemetery.

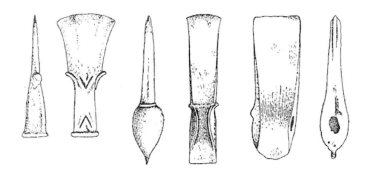

Pantalica. Early Iron Age (1000 B.C.) From Brea, op. cit.

Pantalica. Early Iron Age (1000 B.C.) from Brea, op. cit.

135

Neolithic/5th-4th millennium B.C. 1. Fragments of trichrome pottery. Bronze Age (2nd millennium). 2. Small temple model. 3 Small amphora, 4. Bronze spear cusps. Photohistory/Native Culture. 5. Bullock, bronze (7th-6th c. B.C.). 6. Vase with painted decorations (6th-5th c. B.C.) 7. Vase with painted decorations (6th c. B.C.). 8. Pythos (6th c. B.C.) (Courtesy of Museo Archeologico, Palermo).

The Church of Santa Maria dello Spasimo, after restauration. (Courtesy of Federica DeBellis).

The central nave in the Church of Santa Maria dello Spasimo. (Courtesy of Federica DeBellis).

Via Cavour, Palermo. Final restaurations. (Courtesy of Federica DeBellis).

Civil architecture in Piazza Marina. Palazzo Chiaramonte, also known as Steri, is visible at the end. (Courtesy of Federica DeBellis).

Politeama Theatre, after restaurations. (Courtesy of Federica DeBellis).

The Teatro Massimo in Palermo, after restaurations. (Courtesy of Federica DeBellis).

140